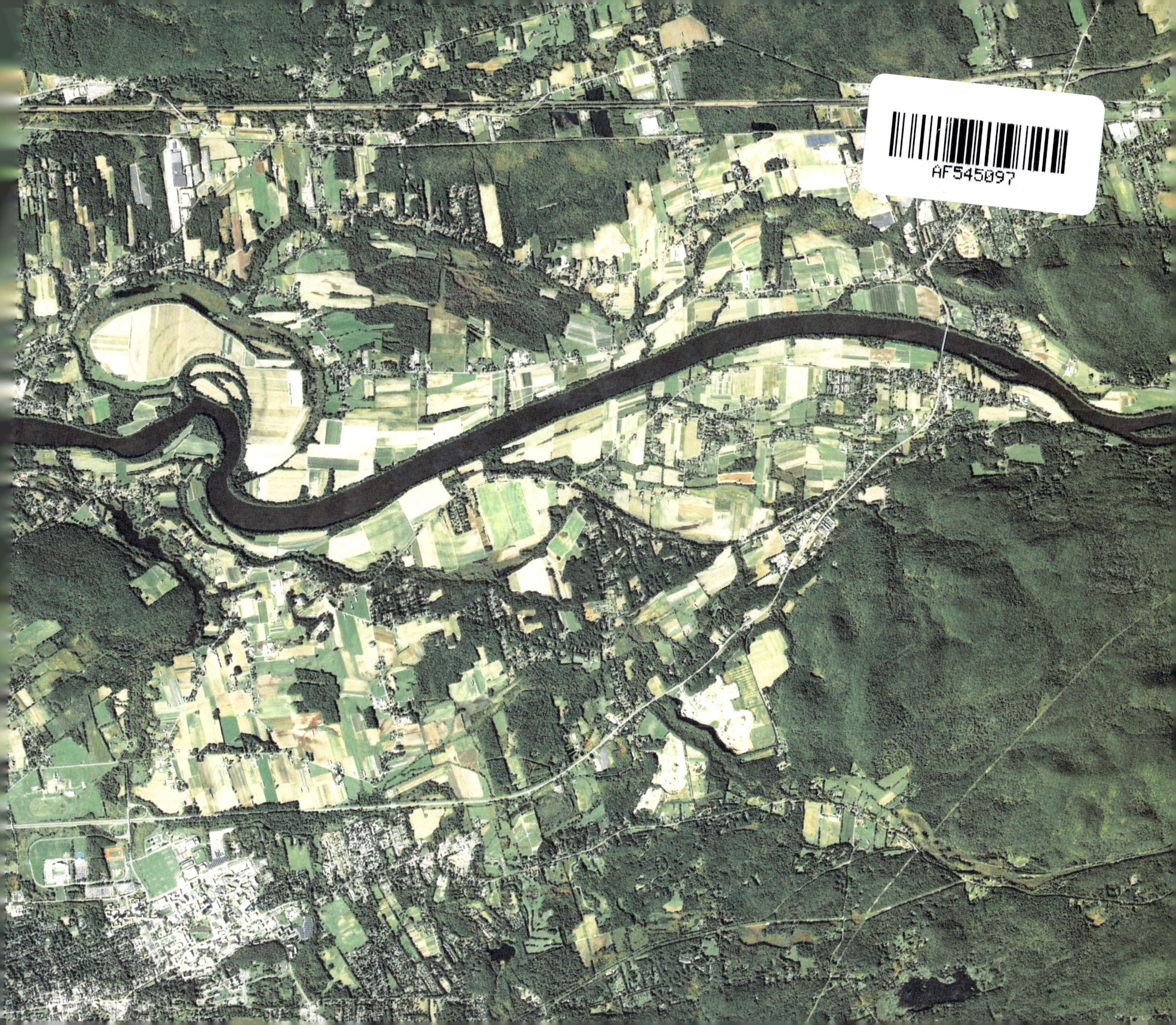

Occupying Massachusetts

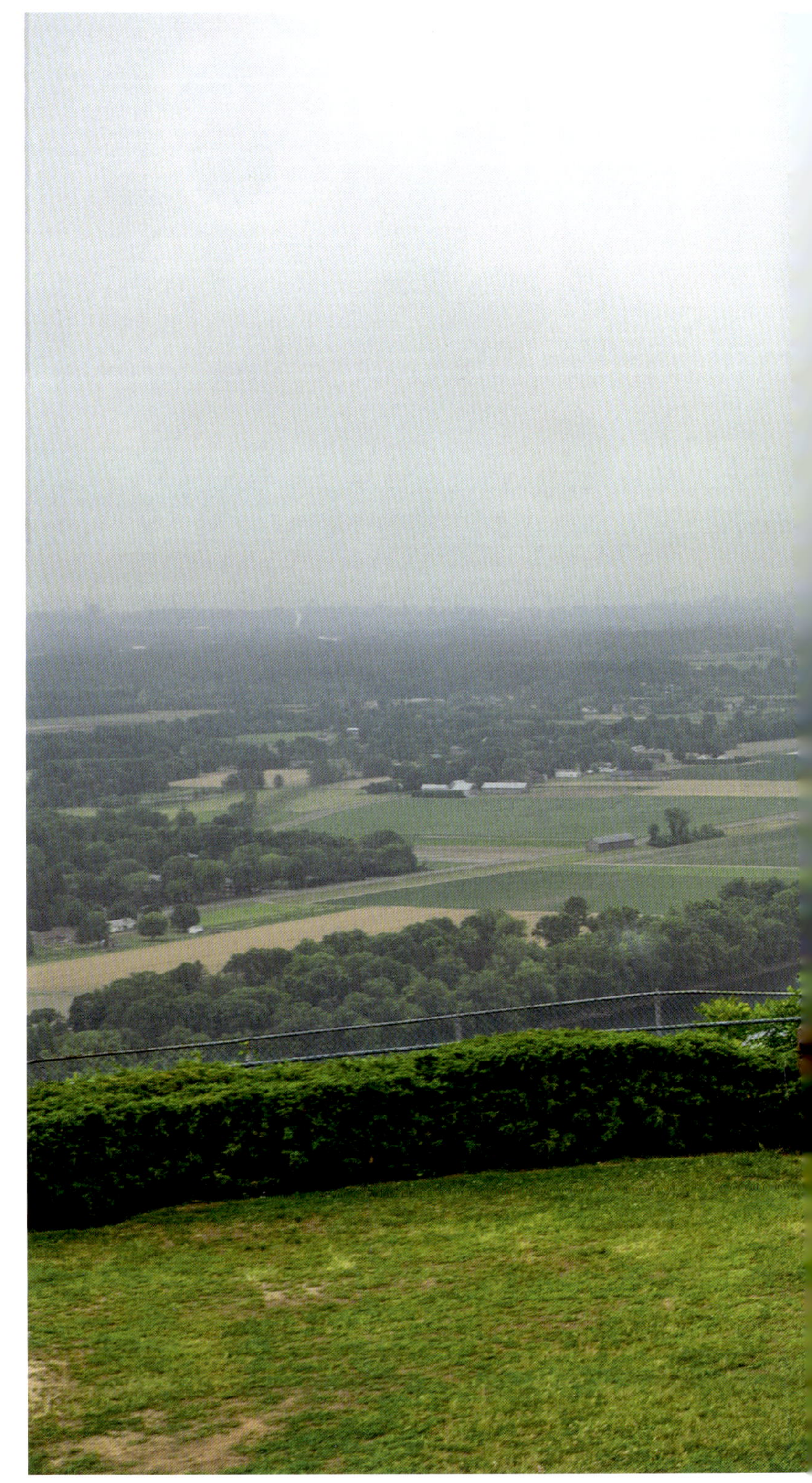

On Nipmuc and Pocumtuck homelands. Overlooking the Connecticut/Kwinitekw River from Mount Sugarloaf, also known as Wequamps, 2020.

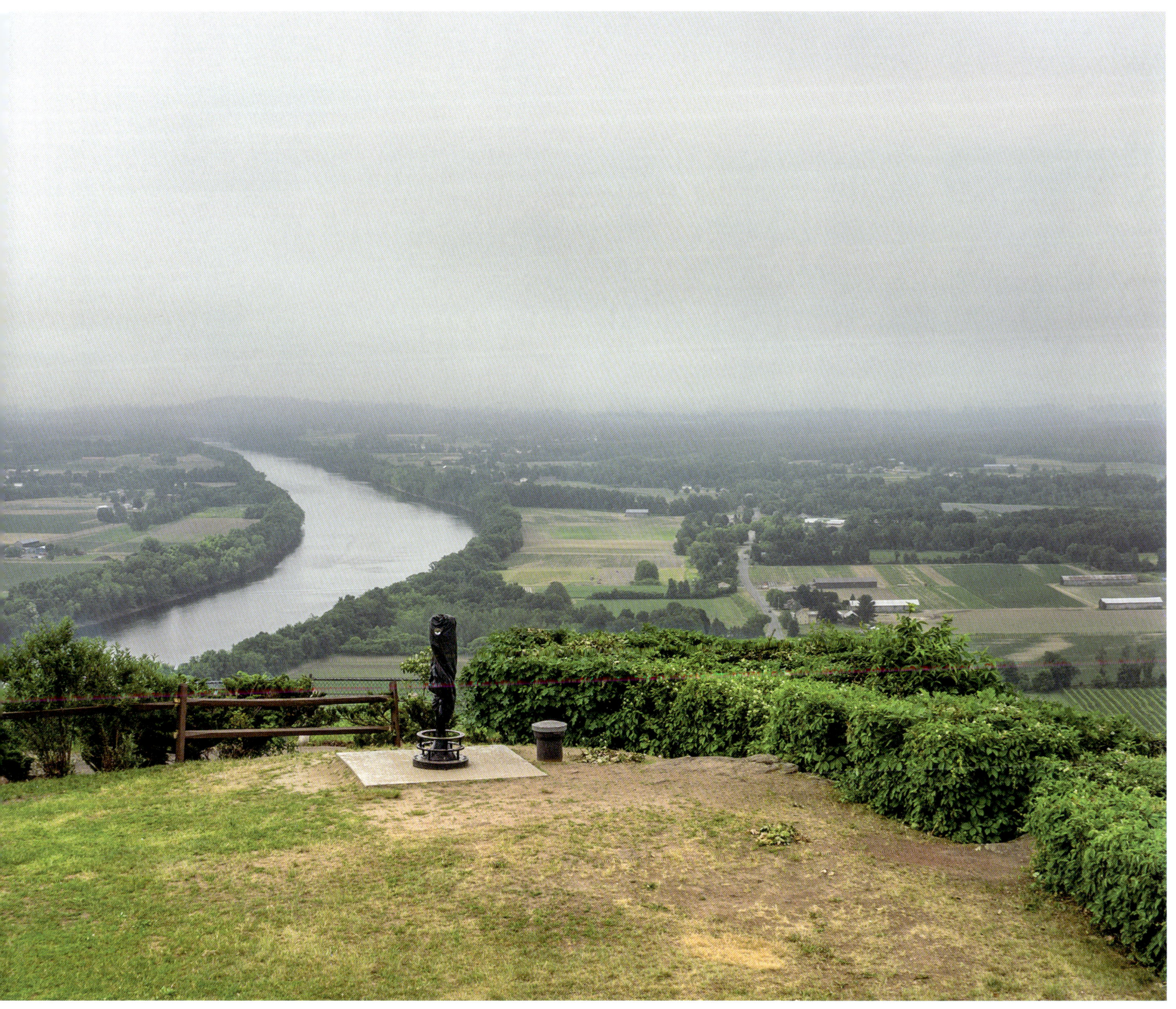

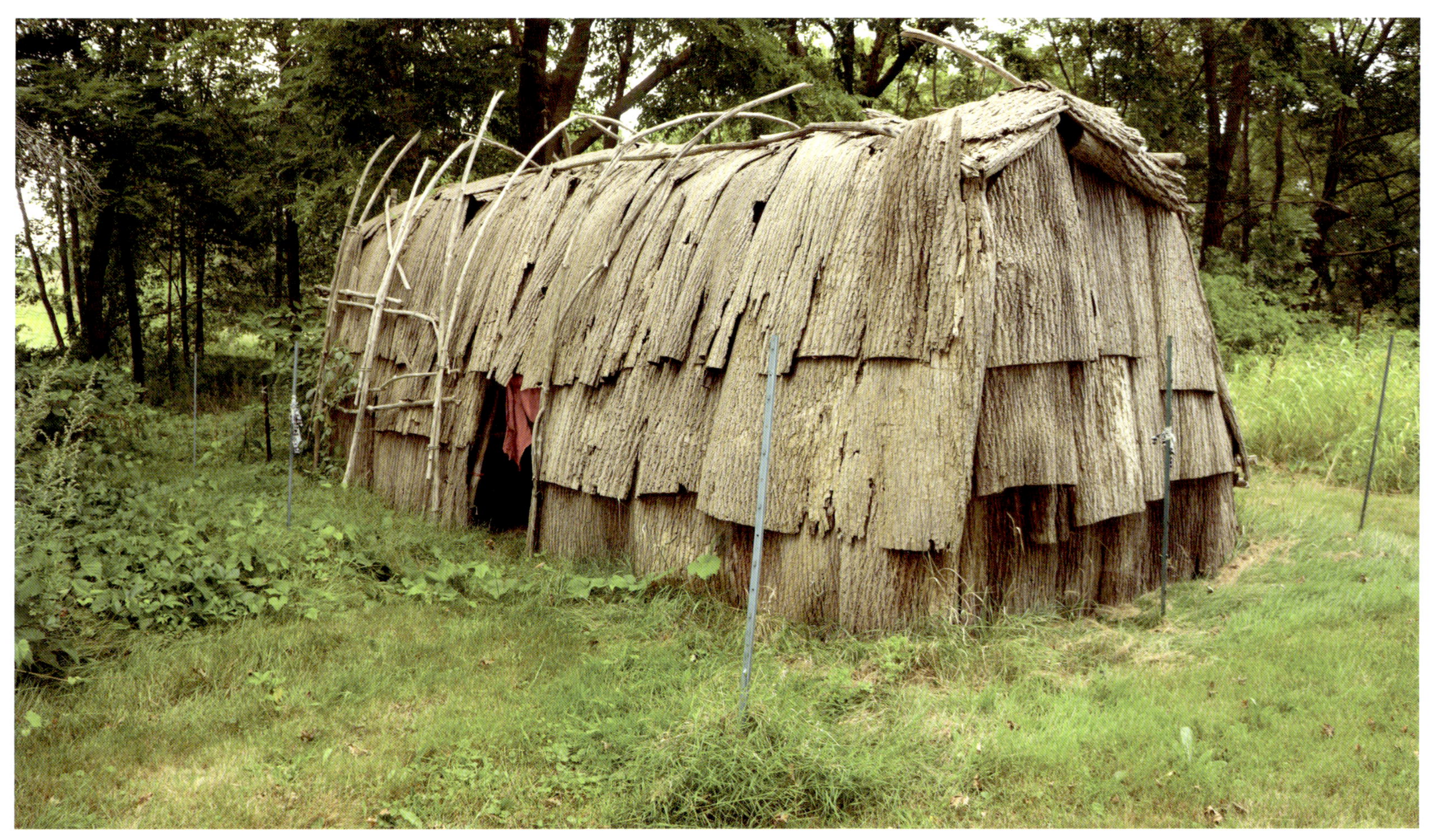

On Pentucket/Pawtucket homelands. A traditional *wetu*, constructed for educational purposes. Ipswich, 2017.

Occupying Massachusetts
Layers of History on Indigenous Land

Sandra Matthews
with texts by David Brule and Suzanne Gardinier

George F. Thompson Publishing
in association with the
Center for the Study of Place

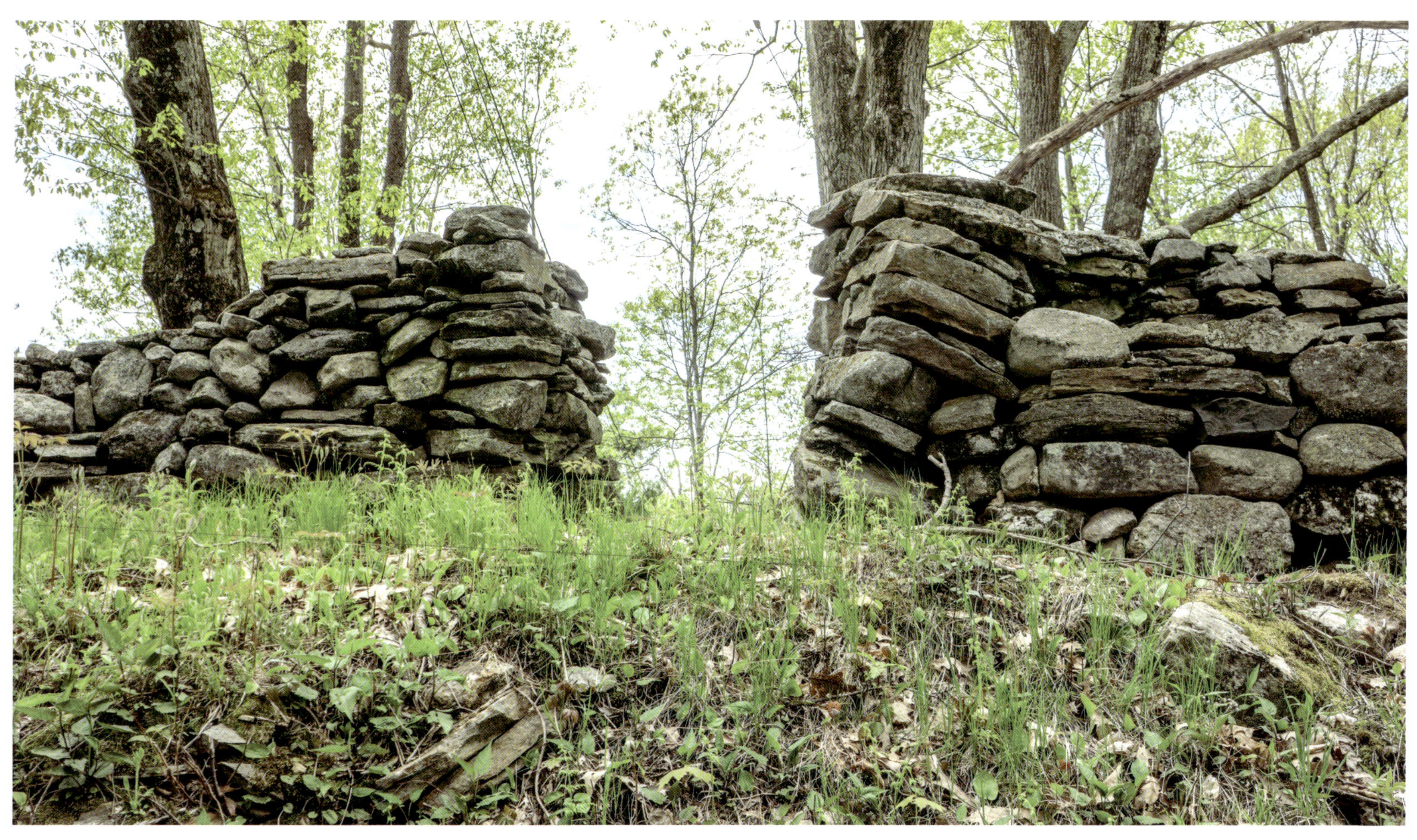

On Nipmuc and Pocumtuck homelands. A New England stone wall,
built in 1806. Shutesbury, also known as Kingyiwngwalak, 2020.

"... a place never belongs to one group: there are always multiple claimants, passers-through, and understandings of the same physical setting."

—CHRISTINE M. DELUCIA, *MEMORY LANDS: KING PHILIP'S WAR AND THE PLACE OF VIOLENCE IN THE NORTHEAST* (2018)

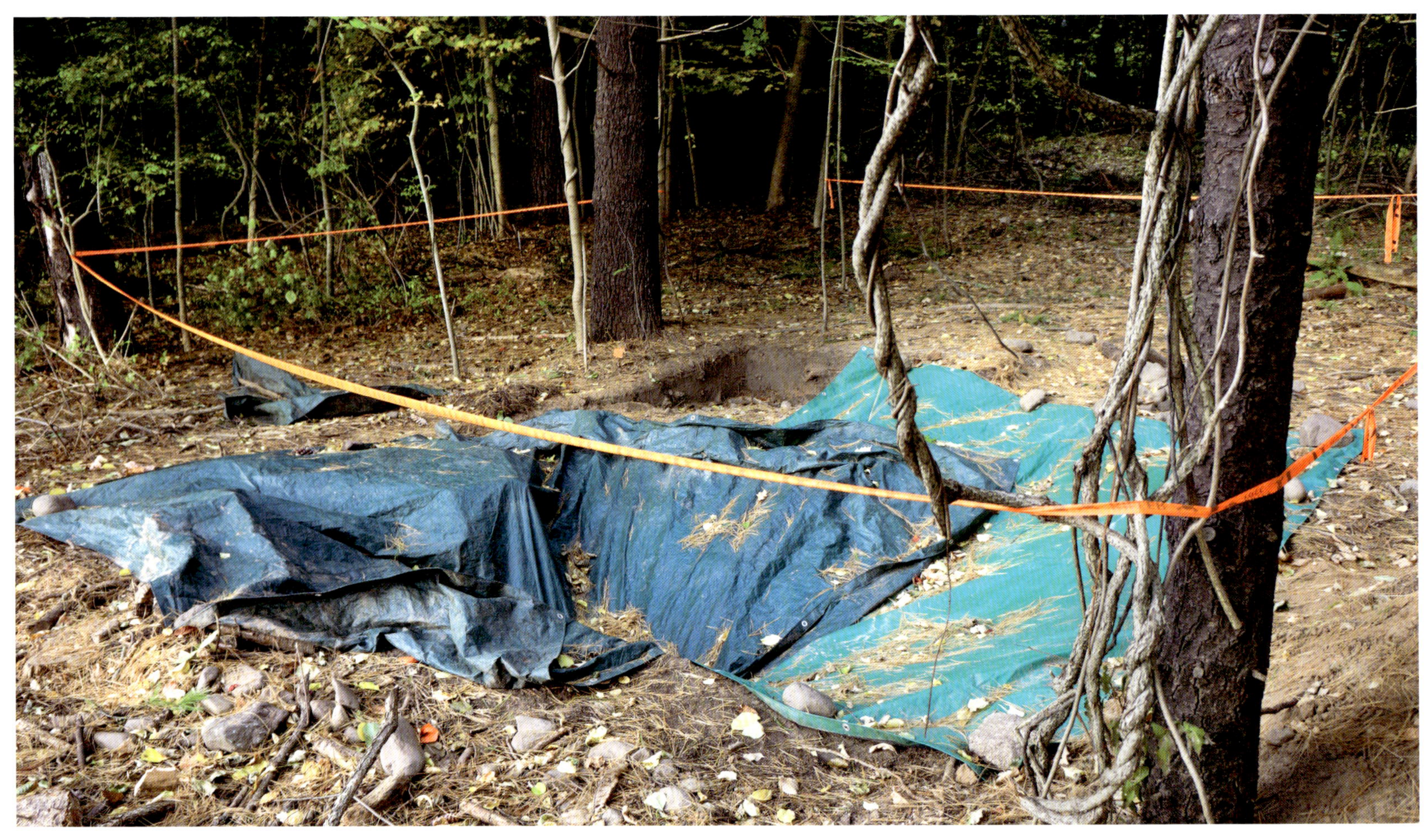

On Nipmuc and Pocumtuck homelands. Site of an Indigenous settlement from the Archaic period, ca. 6000 BCE. Northampton, also known as Nonotuck, 2020.

Introduction

SANDRA MATTHEWS

Massachusetts— where I have lived, with few interruptions, for more than 40 years—is celebrated for its importance in American history. Like most U.S. schoolchildren, I was taught about the Pilgrims, the Puritans, and the Minutemen and taken to visit well-preserved houses from the seventeenth, eighteenth, and nineteenth centuries. But Massachusetts has been inhabited for more than 13,000 years, and people have been building shelters and fashioning sites of meaning on its land since long before the United States of America was even imagined. Although early Indigenous structures can be challenging to find, they are present throughout the state, as are the more than 94,000 people of Indigenous descent who currently make Massachusetts their home.

This book features photographs of idiosyncratic human constructions: domestic, agricultural, religious, and commercial structures made of wood, stone, plastic, brick, or metal. Among them are sheds, animal houses, and trailers placed on the land as well as mysterious constructions whose purposes may be more puzzling. Many are at miniature scale, modeling the essential elements of "home," "shelter," or "settlement." Interspersed are photographs of ancient Indigenous structures and *wetuash*—traditional Algonquian dwellings—here built for teaching and ceremonial purposes rather than for habitation. Made at different points in time, these vernacular constructions all seem to coexist peacefully, but they also hint at past conflicts and struggles and remind us that to build a structure is to assert a claim on territory and on culture.

The Indigenous peoples who occupied Massachusetts for millennia—including the Abenaki, Massachusett, Mohican, Nipmuc, Pawtucket, Pentucket (Pennacook), Pocumtuck, and Wampanoag, whose lands are featured in this book—were joined, during the seventeenth century, by British and European settlers and traders, many of whom also brought with them enslaved Africans. For more than four centuries, people have made their way to Massachusetts from many countries, among them Armenia, Brazil, Cambodia, China, Congo, El Salvador, France, Haiti, India, Ireland, Italy, and Poland, often leaving their homelands for reasons of persecution, war, famine, or extreme poverty. Many stories can be told about individuals and ethnic groups who came to Massachusetts and struggled to make places for themselves, but, in this book, their stories are secondary to the underlying narrative of the expulsion of Indigenous people from their homelands.

To the extent that the United States can offer a haven to people from outside its borders—as it did to my own immigrant parents—that offer is built, tragically, on the original violent displacement of Indigenous peoples in Massachusetts and throughout the nation. In her powerful meditation, "Notes of a Settler Daughter" (pages 81–85), Suzanne Gardinier, who was born in New Bedford, Massachusetts, and raised in Scituate, Massachusetts, vividly enumerates the continuing effects of this traumatic history, placing it in the context of other genocides and dispossessions worldwide.

Texts from eleven historical markers, selected from hundreds around the state, appear throughout the book. The markers describe interactions between Indigenous people and early settlers, offering fragmentary narratives written from distinct—mostly non-Indigenous—points of view. Emphasis is on the events of King Philip's War (1675–1676), during which, with heavy losses on both sides, the English colonists, far outnumbering Indigenous people, took decisive control of the land. The tone and content of these historical markers reflect the interests of their makers. The physical markers themselves also have stories, as they are refurbished, defaced, or allowed to "age in place." Indigenous ceremonial stone sites generally do not have signage, marking history with their presence in other ways.

In his thoughtful essay, "Occupying Indigenous Land: Finding a Way Forward" (pages 75–77), David Brule, who was born and raised in Montague, Massachusetts, writes about the importance of making space for all stories to be heard. Occupying land is a basic human activity; people seek to make themselves at home in the world and build structures to fulfill that desire. But when land is taken by force and deception, the narratives accompanying such an occupation are especially potent. Such narratives, found on historical markers and in many other places, can enable and justify violence, twist and suppress other versions of the story, and perpetuate harm far into the future.

This book intertwines the theme of "occupation" with questions about the telling of history: How do people occupy land? How is the story of their occupation told? As an occupant/occupier of Massachusetts myself, I offer here my pictorial observations together with texts of different kinds, in the hope they will invite reflection about difficult histories, the fleeting nature of "home," cultural survival, and the ongoing relationships between people and the land, as seen in the structures we make.

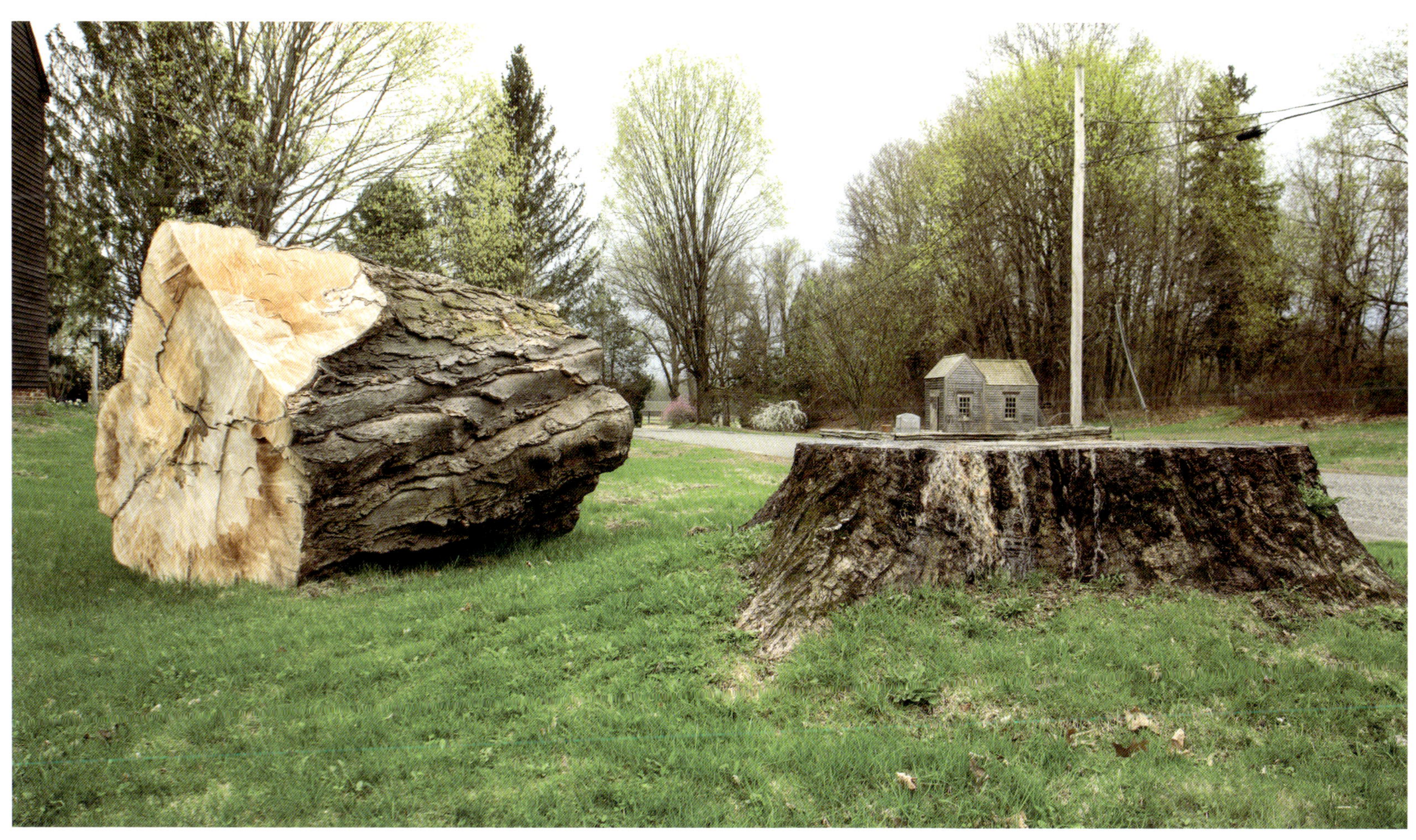

On Nipmuc and Pocumtuck homelands. Hatfield, also known as Capawonk, 2019.

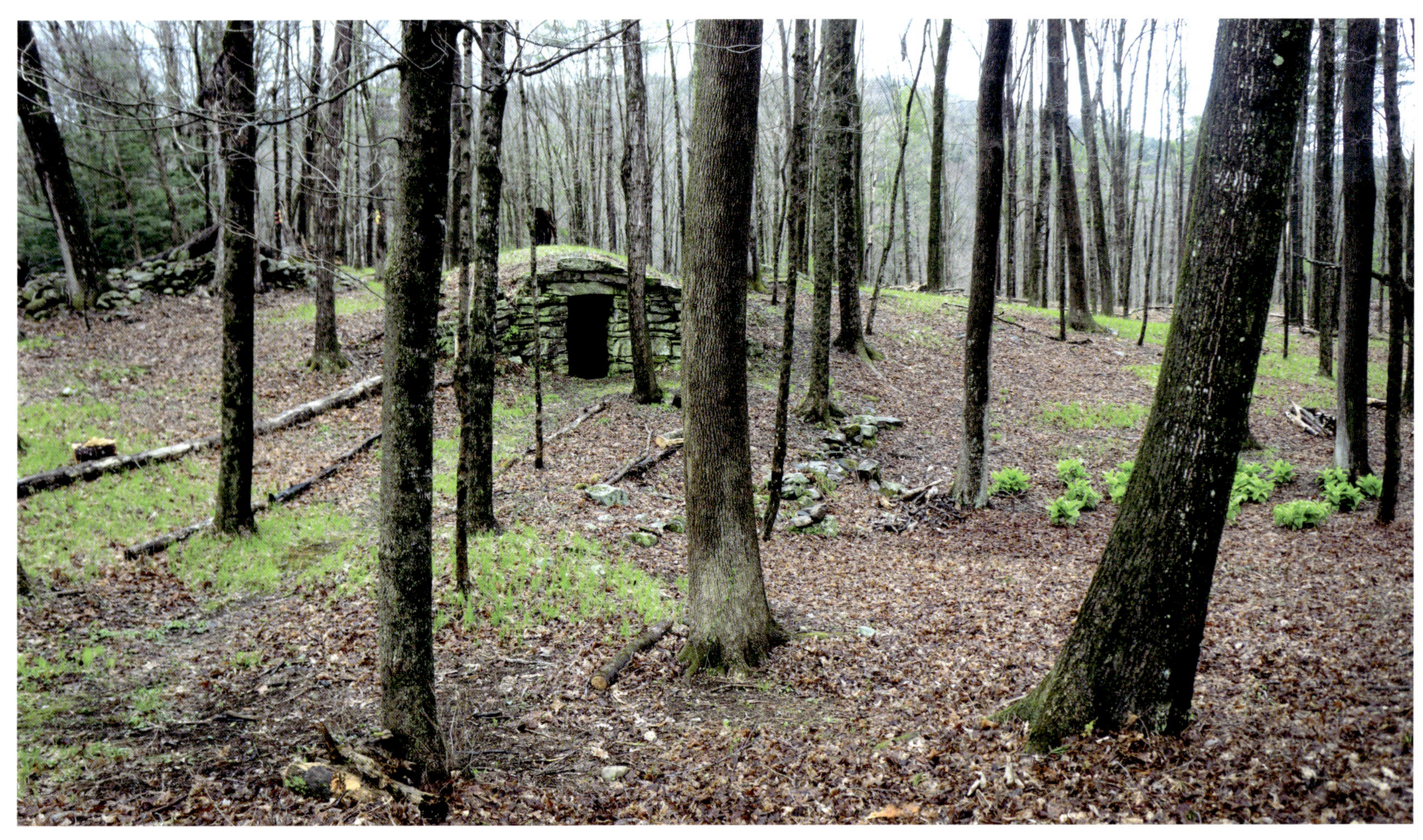

On Nipmuc and Pocumtuck homelands. Stone chamber, date and origin unknown. Leverett, 2018.

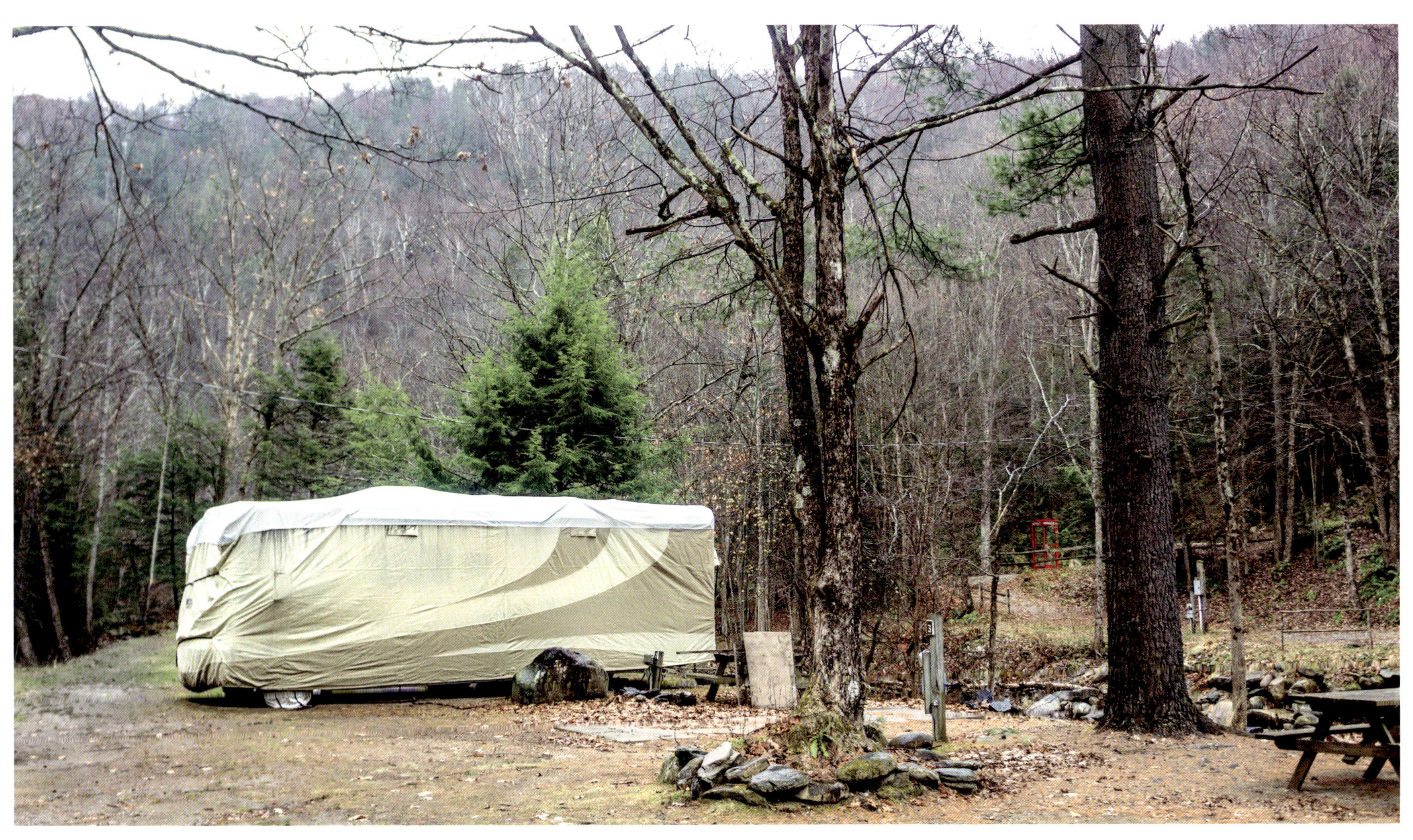

On Pocumtuck and Mohican homelands. Chester, 2017.

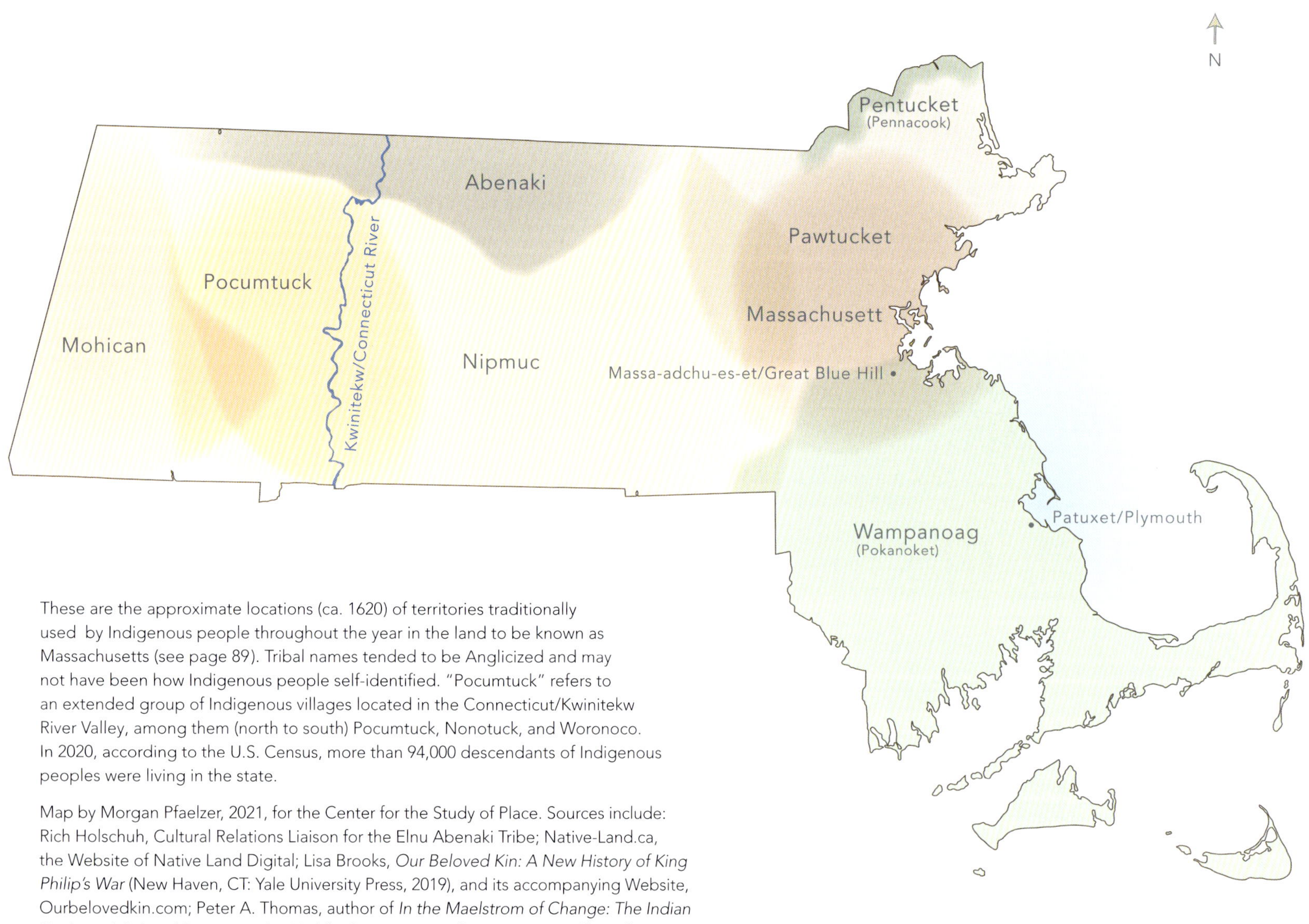

These are the approximate locations (ca. 1620) of territories traditionally used by Indigenous people throughout the year in the land to be known as Massachusetts (see page 89). Tribal names tended to be Anglicized and may not have been how Indigenous people self-identified. "Pocumtuck" refers to an extended group of Indigenous villages located in the Connecticut/Kwinitekw River Valley, among them (north to south) Pocumtuck, Nonotuck, and Woronoco. In 2020, according to the U.S. Census, more than 94,000 descendants of Indigenous peoples were living in the state.

Map by Morgan Pfaelzer, 2021, for the Center for the Study of Place. Sources include: Rich Holschuh, Cultural Relations Liaison for the Elnu Abenaki Tribe; Native-Land.ca, the Website of Native Land Digital; Lisa Brooks, *Our Beloved Kin: A New History of King Philip's War* (New Haven, CT: Yale University Press, 2019), and its accompanying Website, Ourbelovedkin.com; Peter A. Thomas, author of *In the Maelstrom of Change: The Indian Trade and Cultural Process in the Middle Connecticut Valley, 1635–1665* (Shrewsbury, MA: Garland Press, 1991); and *The Smithsonian Handbook of North American Indians, Volume 15: Northeast* (Washington, DC: Smithsonian Institution, 1978).

Occupying Massachusetts

SAMUEL DE CHAMPLAIN

DUE EAST FROM HERE ON JULY 16, 1605 THE SIEUR DE MONTS SENT SAMUEL DE CHAMPLAIN ASHORE TO PARLEY WITH SOME INDIANS. THEY DANCED FOR HIM AND TRACED AN OUTLINE MAP OF MASSACHUSETTS BAY . . .

—Marker installed by the Massachusetts Bay Colony Tercentenary Commission in 1930

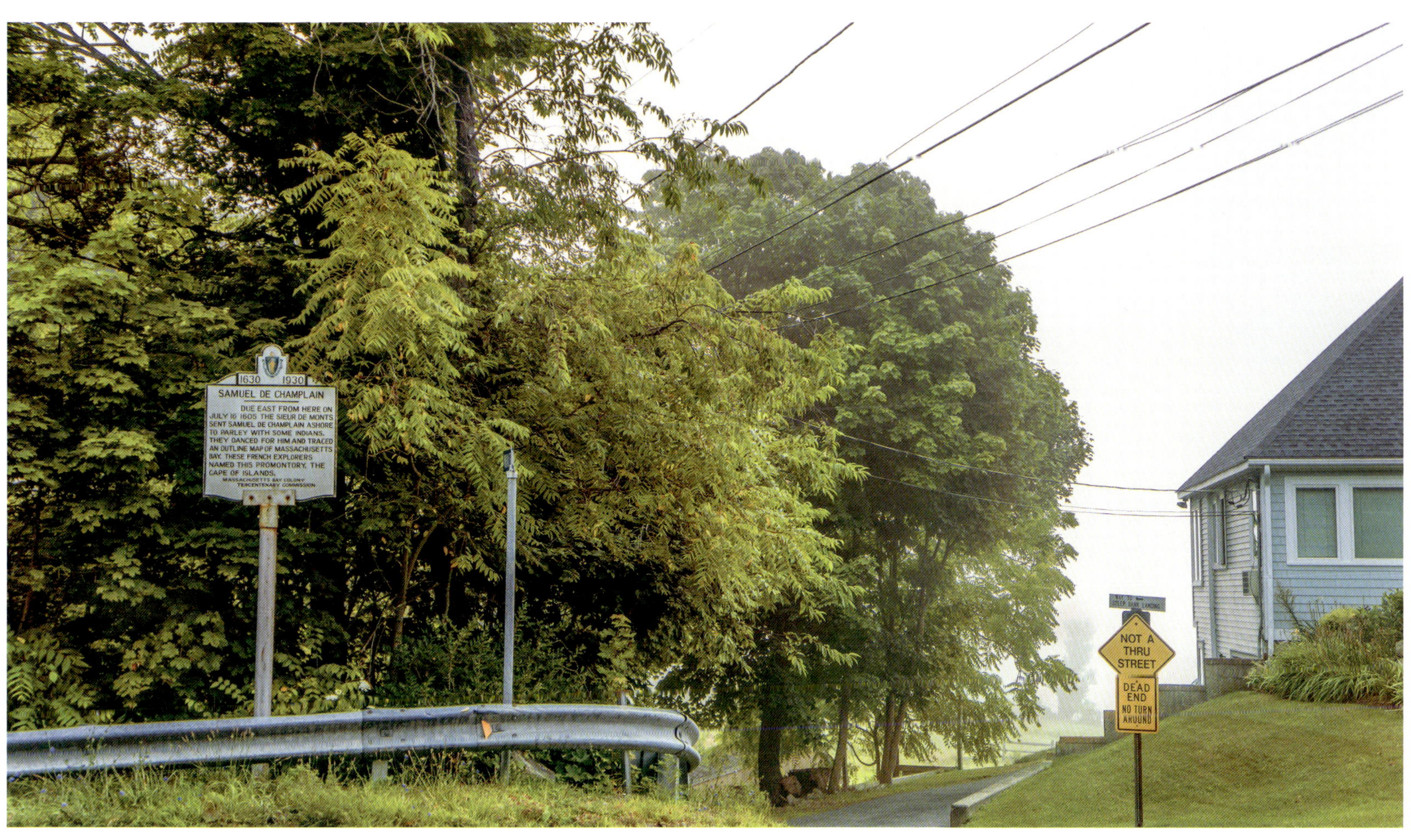

On Pawtucket homelands. Rockport, 2019.

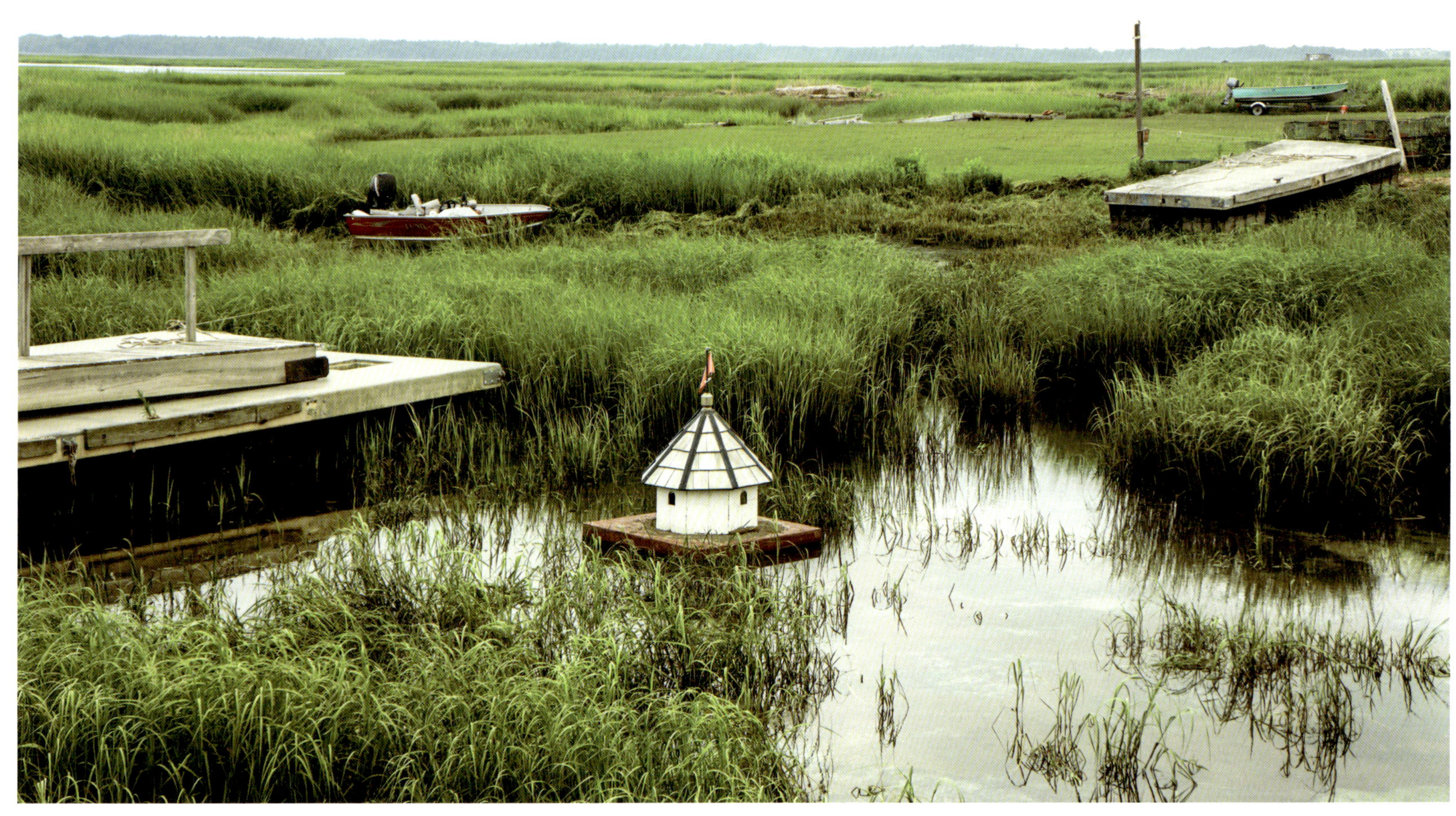

On Pentucket/Pawtucket homelands. Parker River watershed. Newbury, 2015.

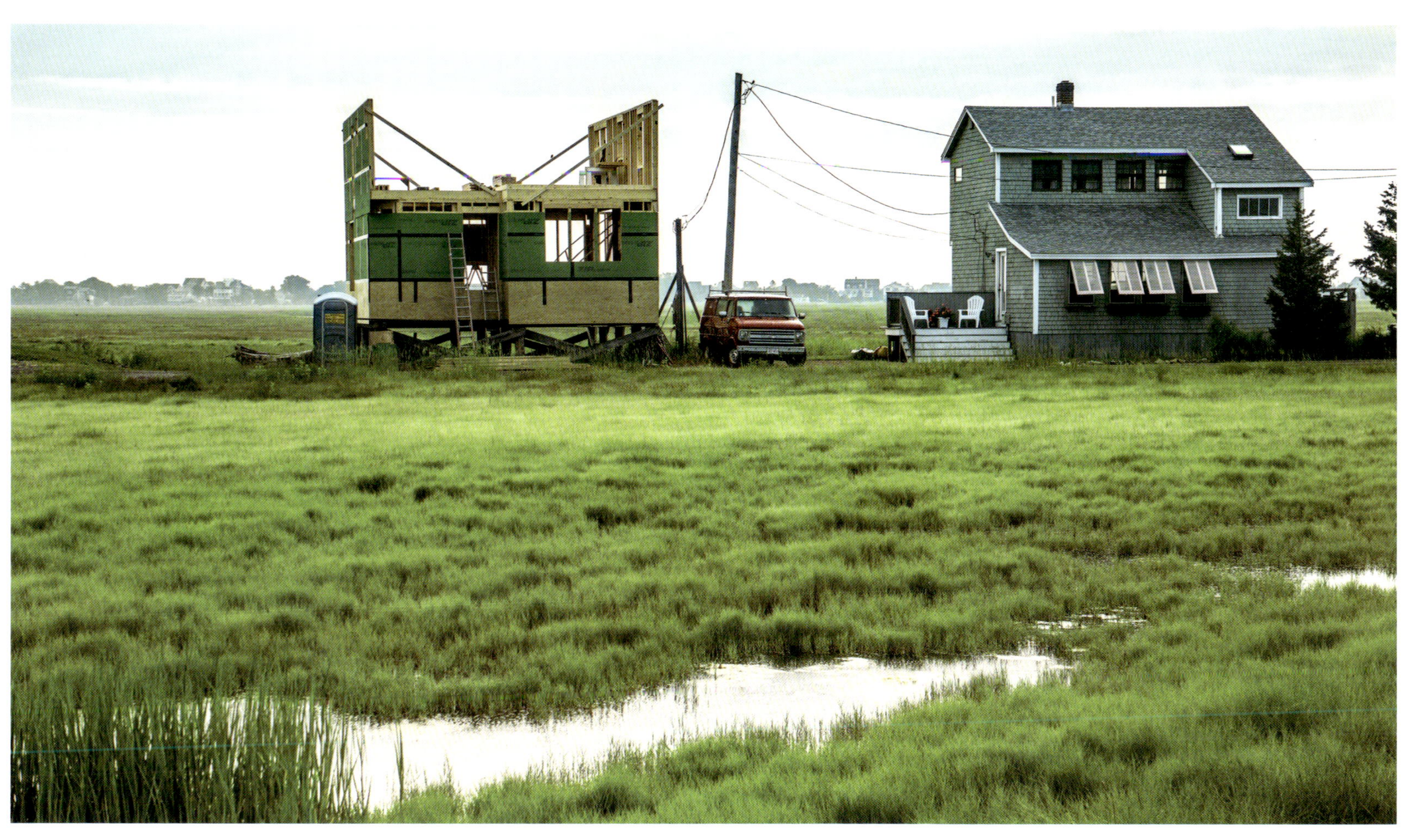

On Pentucket/Pawtucket homelands. Newbury, 2015.

NEWBURY

INDIAN REGION CALLED QUASCACUNQUEN.
SETTLED 1635 UNDER LEADERSHIP OF THE
PURITAN CLERGYMAN THOMAS PARKER.

—Marker installed by the Massachusetts Bay
Colony Tercentenary Commission in 1930

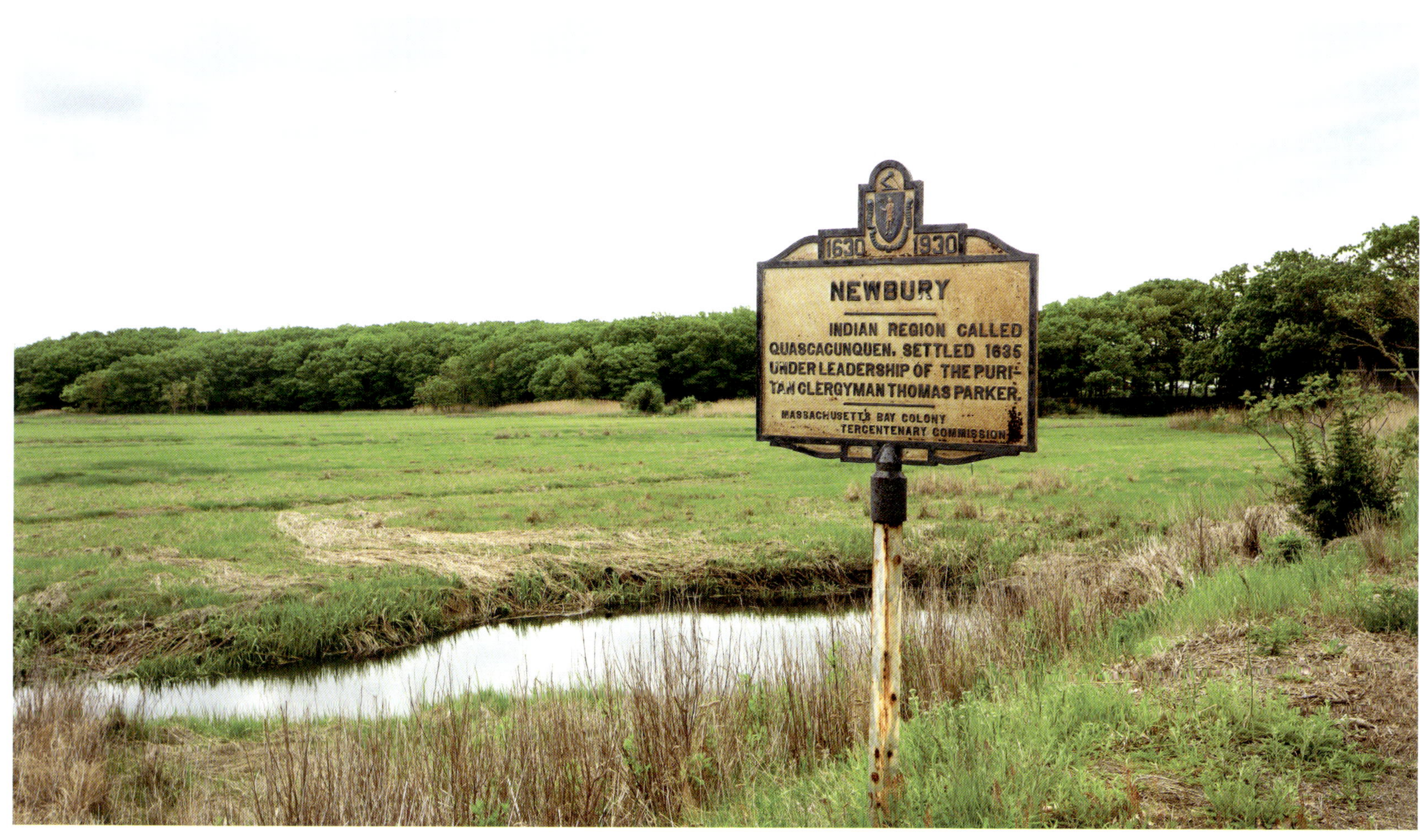

On Pentucket/Pawtucket homelands. Newbury, 2017.

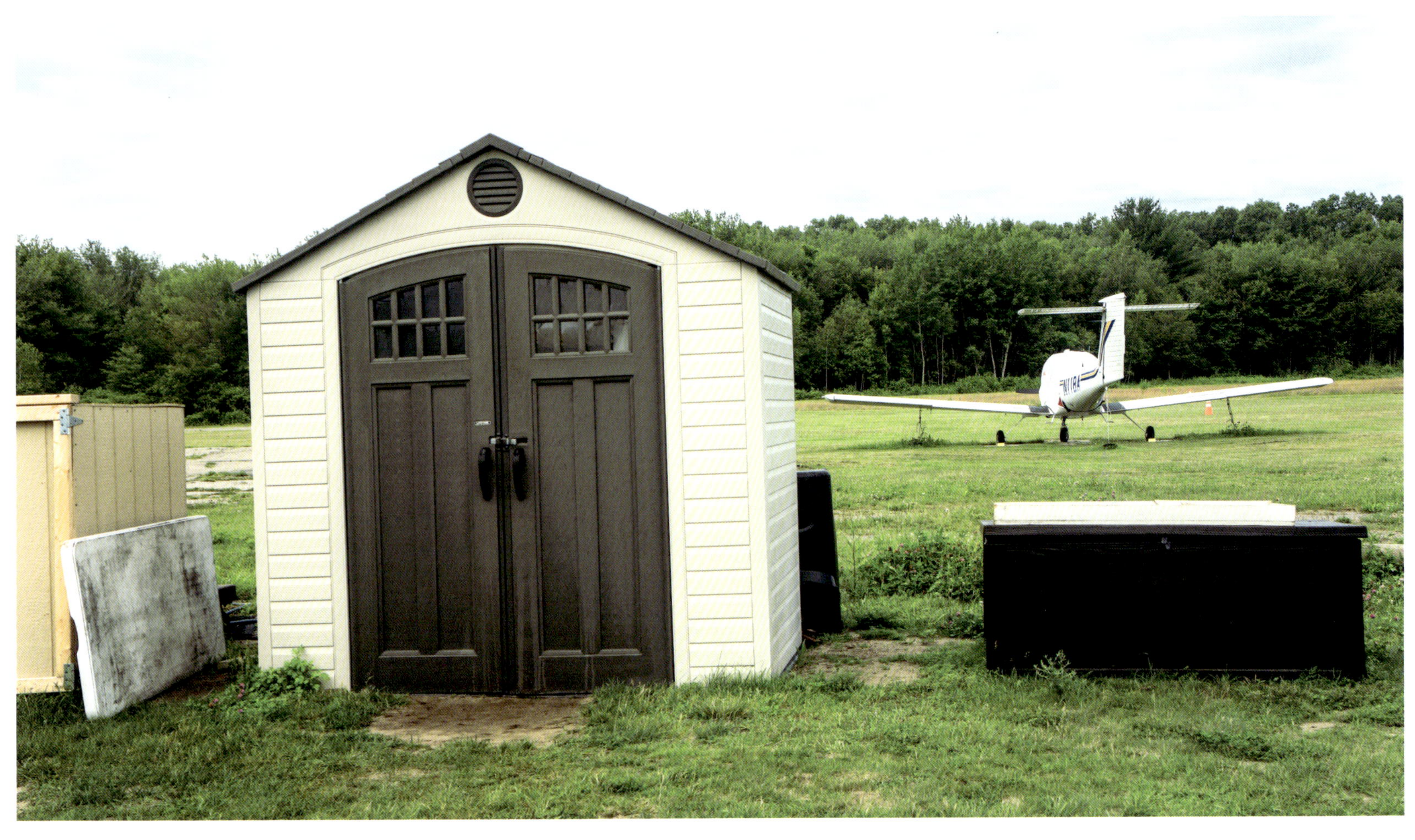

On Pentucket/Pawtucket homelands. Newburyport, 2015.

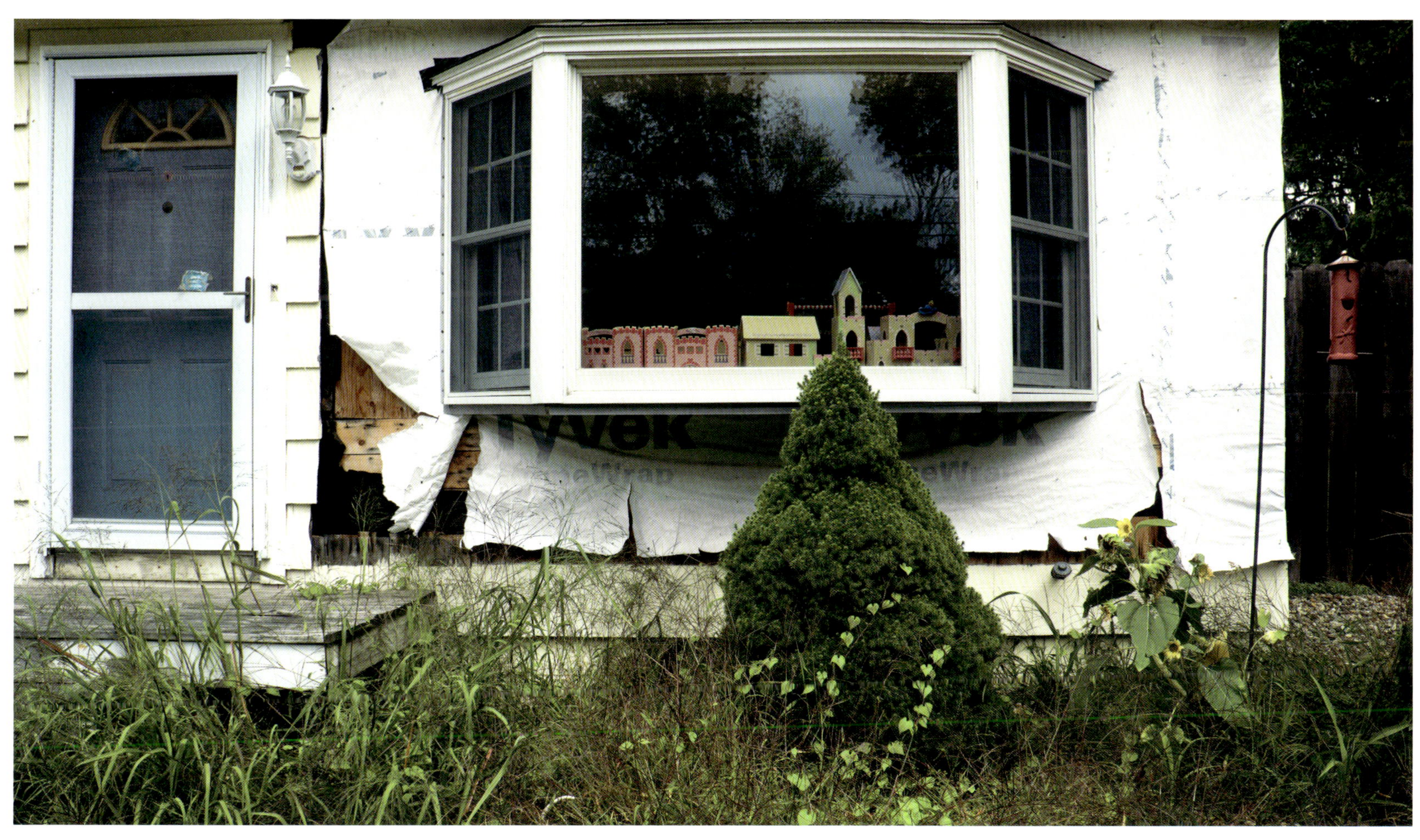

On Pentucket/Pawtucket homelands. Newburyport, 2017.

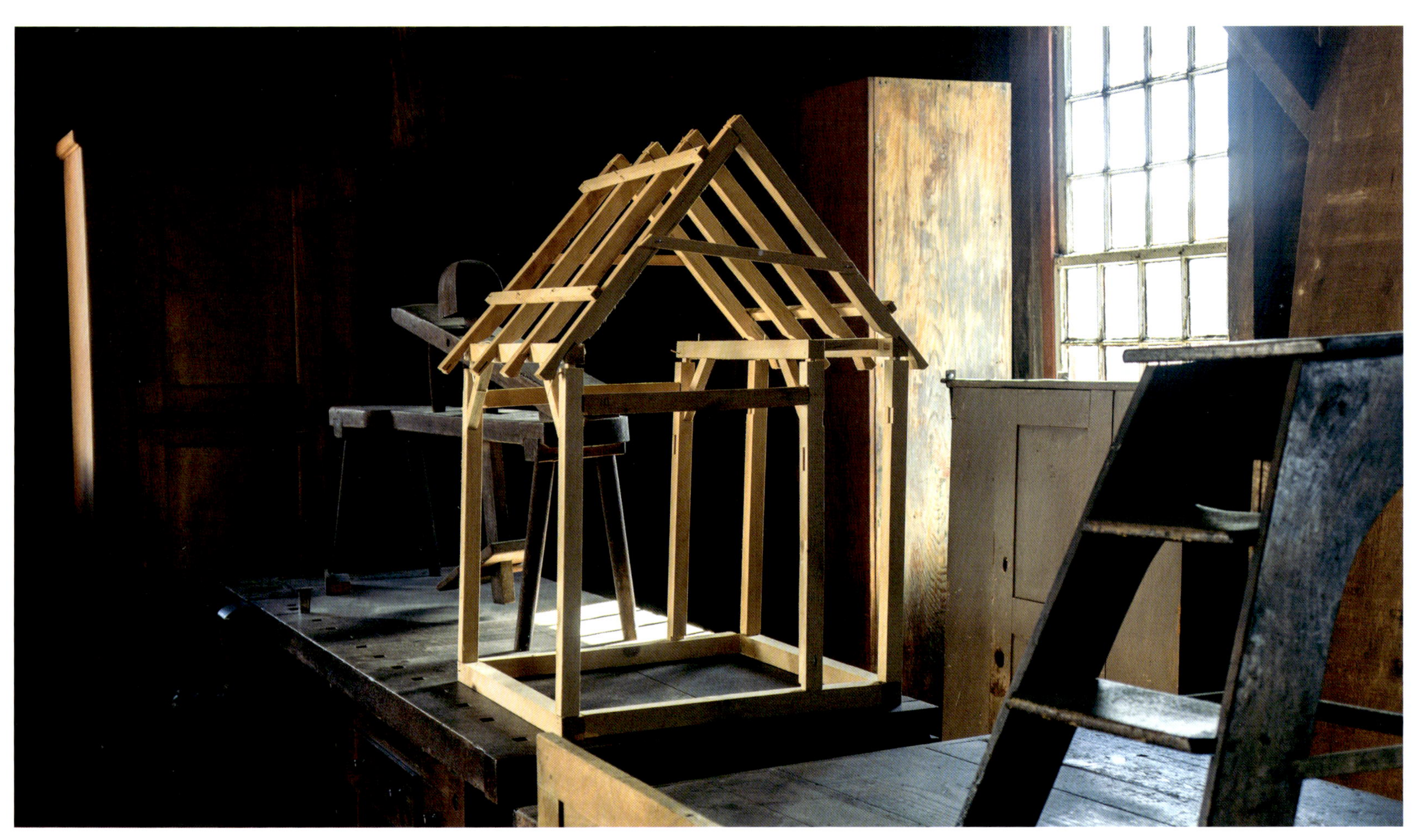

On Mohican homelands. Hancock Shaker Village. Hancock, 2016.

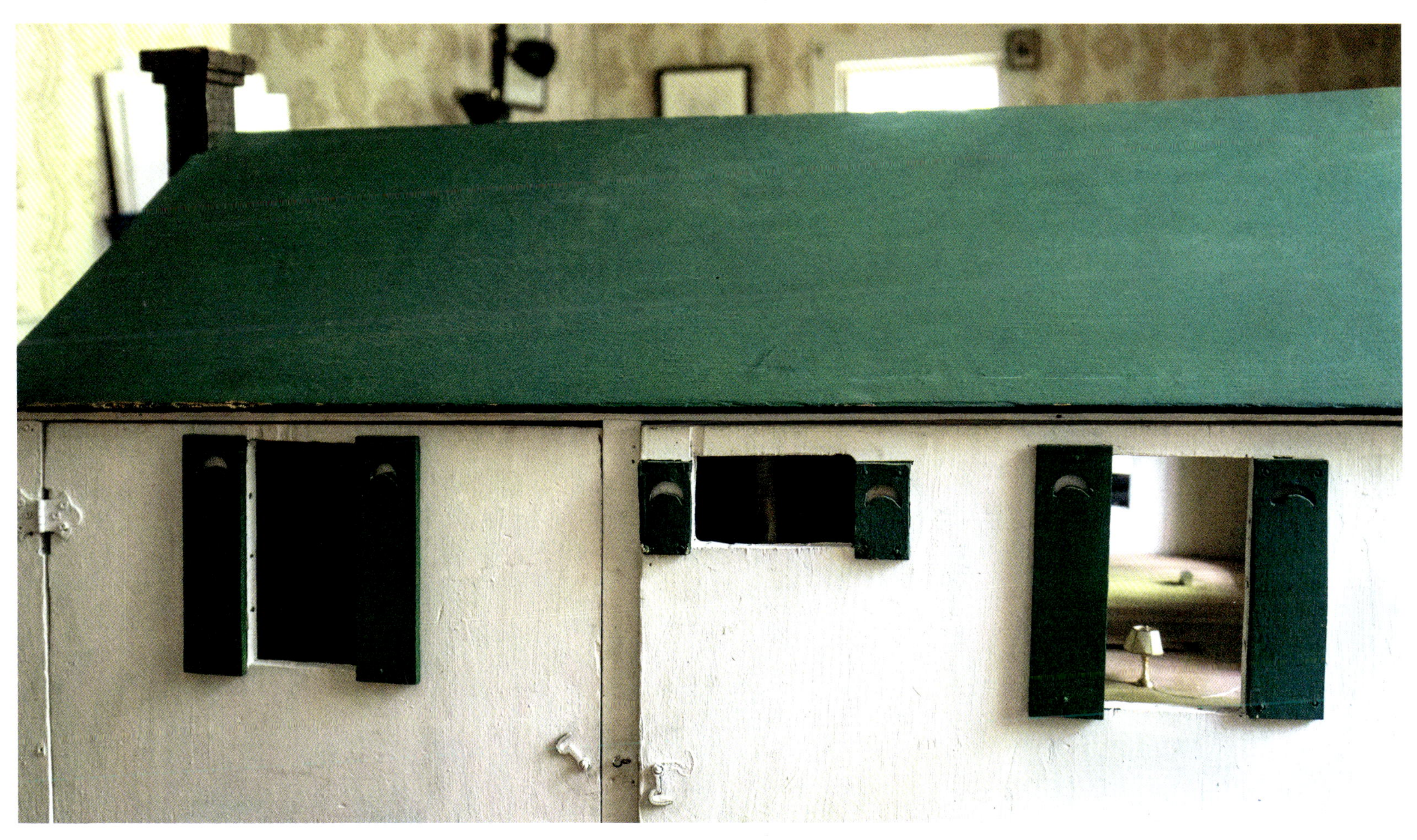

On Nipmuc and Pocumtuck homelands. Northampton/Nonotuck, 2016.

ON THIS SITE JOHN ELIOT HELPED HIS INDIAN CONVERTS TO BUILD THEIR FIRST MEETINGHOUSE IN 1651 WITH A 'PROPHET'S CHAMBER' WHERE HE LODGED ON HIS FORTNIGHTLY VISITS TO PREACH TO THEM IN THEIR LANGUAGE . . .

—Text from a nearby marker, installed by the Massachusetts Bay Colony Tercentenary Commission in 1930.

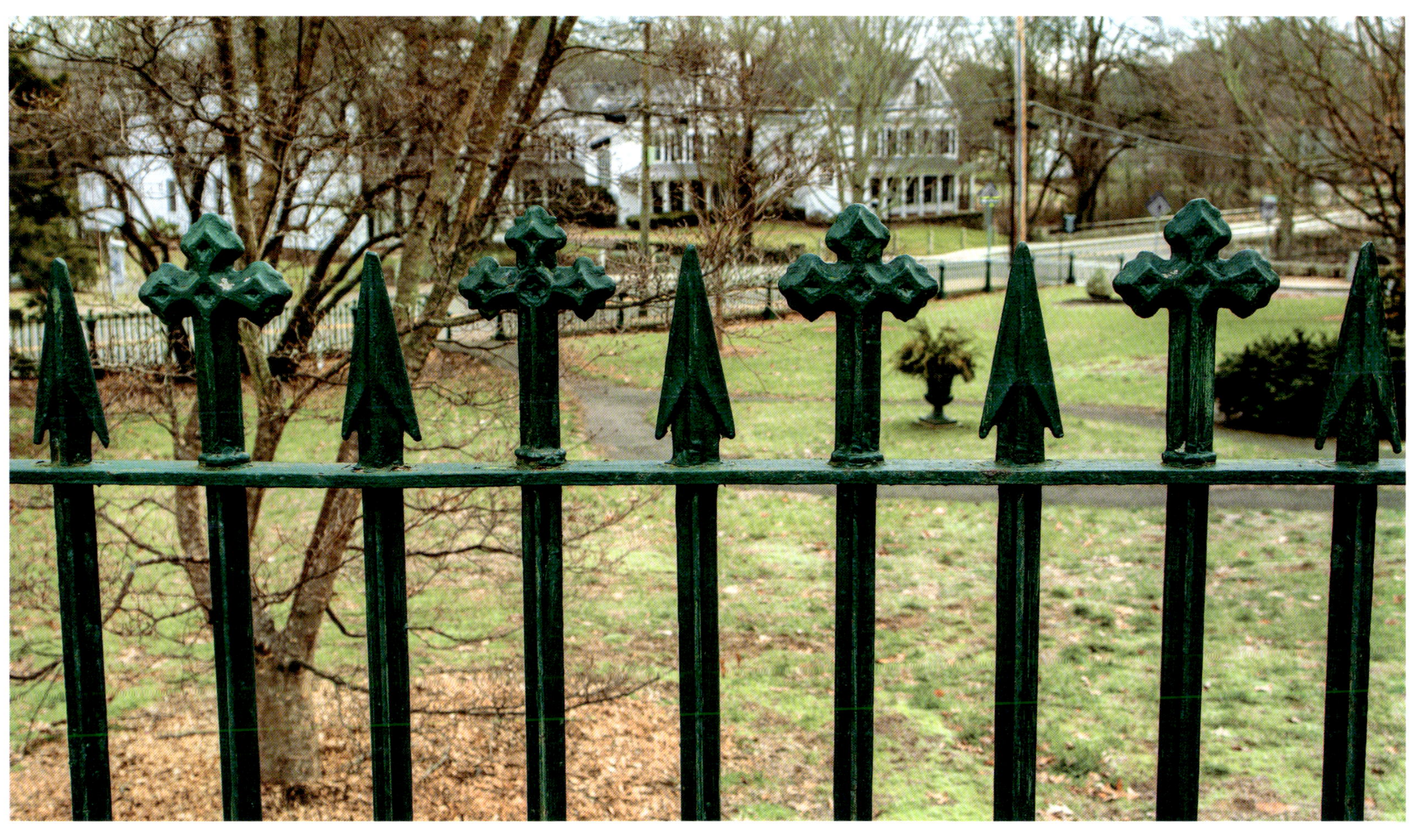

On Massachusett, Nipmuc, and Pentucket/Pawtucket homelands.
Fence alongside a seventeenth-century "Indian Burial Ground." Natick, 2021.

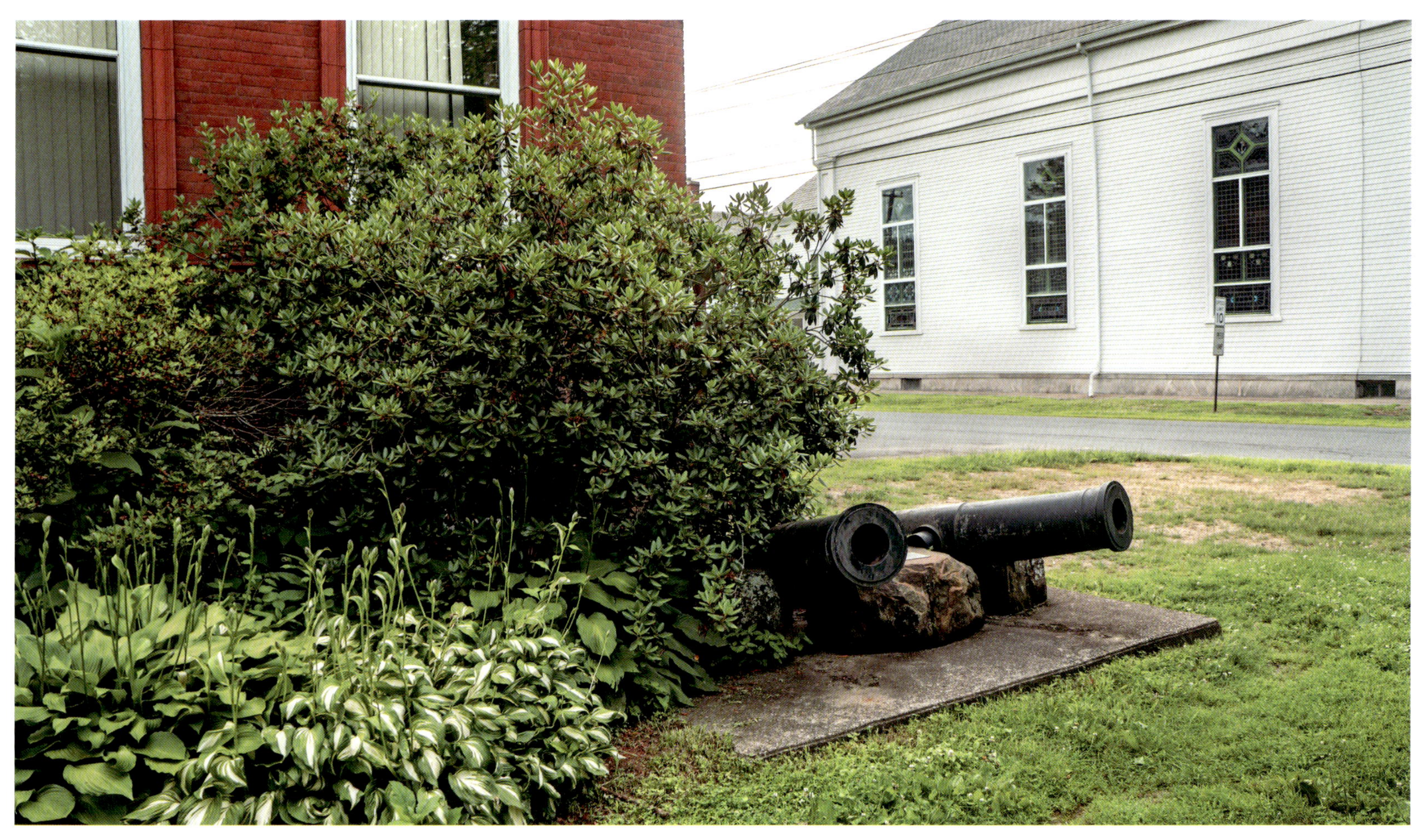

On Nipmuc and Pocumtuck homelands. Hatfield/Capawonk, 2019.

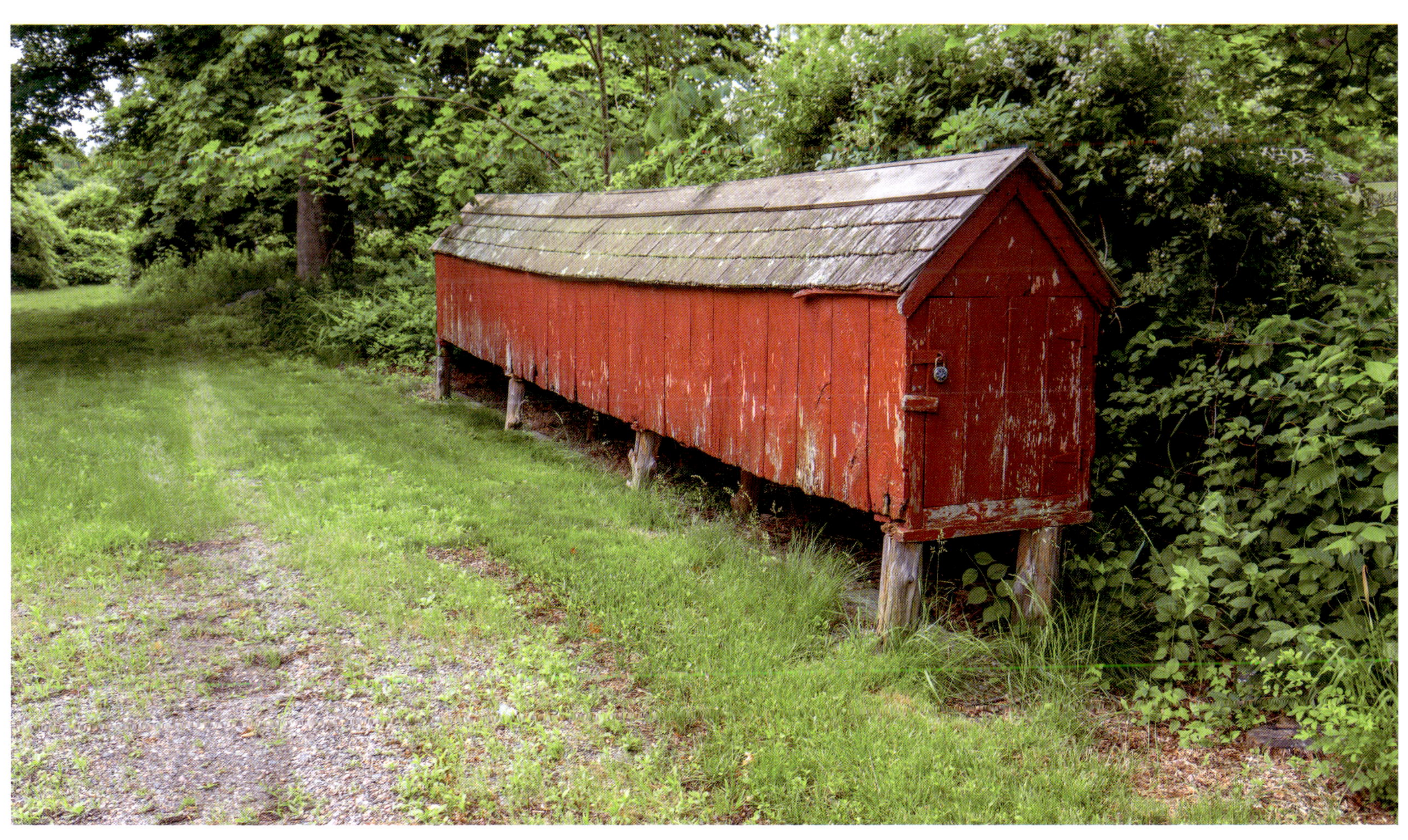

On Pentucket/Pawtucket homelands. Ladder house, ca. 1677. Rowley, 2017.

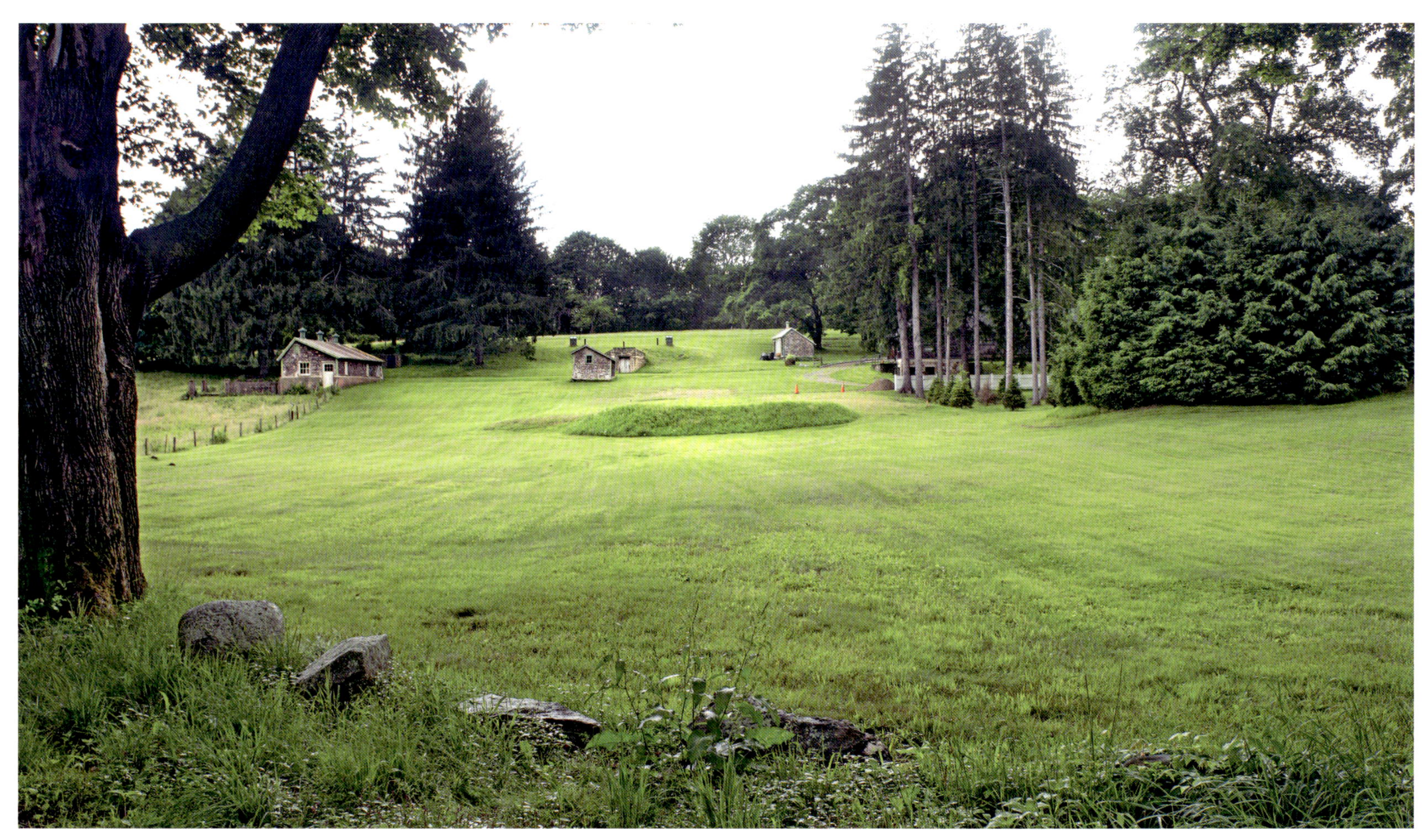

On Pentucket/Pawtucket homelands. Maudslay State Park. Newburyport, 2019.

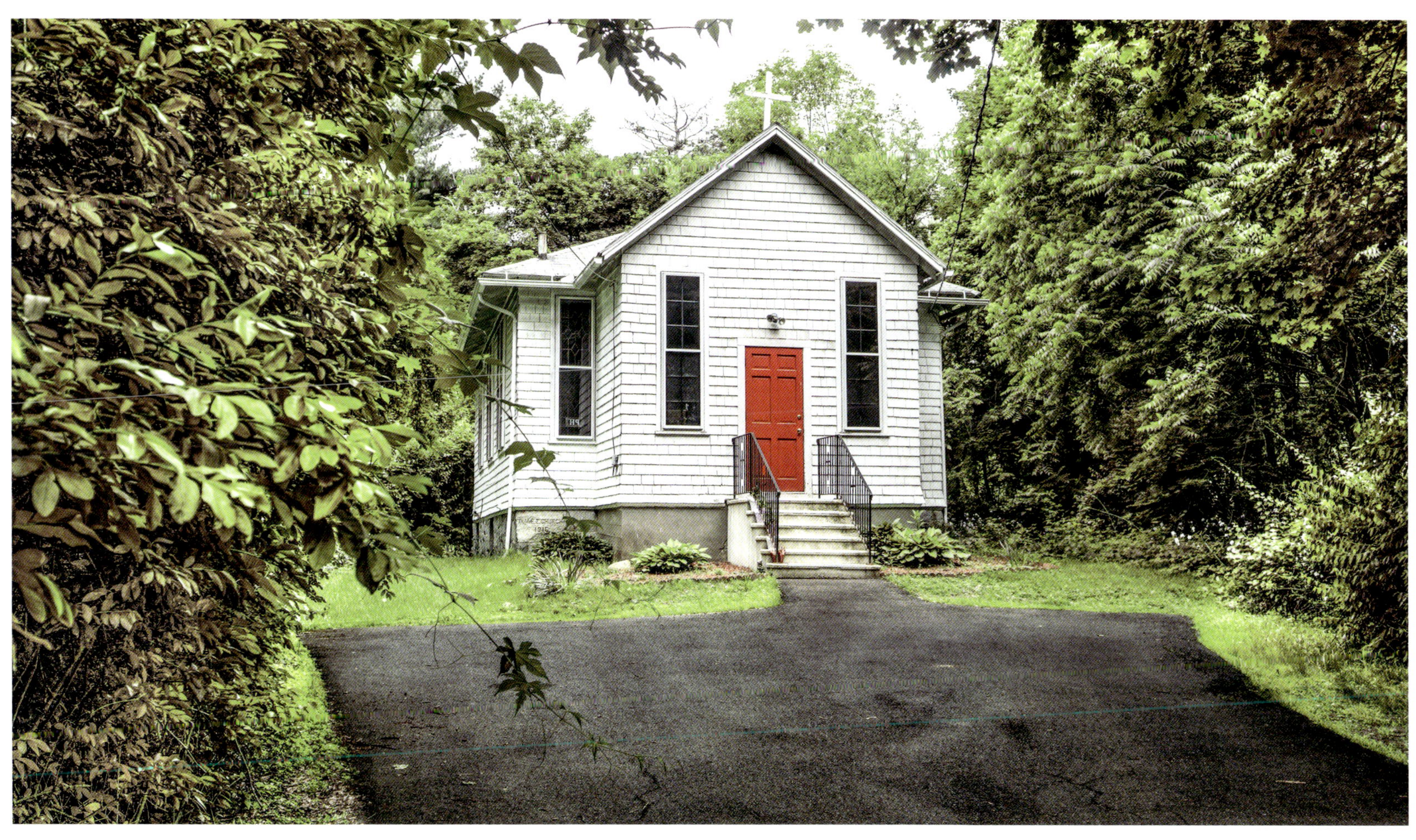

On Nipmuc and Pocumtuck homelands. Goodwin Memorial African Methodist Episcopal Zion Church. Amherst, 2018.

A PEACEFUL BUT POWERFUL SACHEM WHO RULED HIS PEOPLE, THE AGAWAMS, IN THE LANDS OF ESSEX COUNTY FROM NEWBURY TO HAVERHILL TO BEVERLY AND ALL THE CAPE ANN TO THE ATLANTIC OCEAN. THE AGAWAMS WERE DECIMATED BY A PLAGUE LASTING THREE YEARS AROUND 1617, PROBABLY INTRODUCED BY FOREIGN TRADERS ALONG THE 200 MILES OF NORTHEAST COAST.

WHEN JOHN WINTHROP ARRIVED IN WHAT IS NOW 'MANCHESTER-BY-THE-SEA,' IN 1630, MASCONOMET PADDLED OUT TO THE "ARABELLA" TO GREET THE WHITE SETTLERS. HE WAS VERY FRIENDLY AND WAS ABLE TO CONVERSE IN ENGLISH EVEN THOUGH HIS NATIVE TONGUE WAS ALGONQUIN.

BY 1638, THE DWINDLED TRIBE EXISTED MOSTLY IN THE IPSWICH AREA. MASCONOMET SOLD HIS LAND THAT YEAR TO JOHN WINTHROP, JR., FOR 20 POUNDS ENGLISH. SIX YEARS LATER HE REQUESTED INSTRUCTION IN CHRISTIAN WAYS AND ACCEPTED PROTECTION FROM THE MASSACHUSETTS BAY COLONY UNDER A SIGNED AGREEMENT. HE WAS GIVEN 6 ACRES OF PLANTING GROUND IN 1655. THREE YEARS LATER, ON MARCH 6, 1658, HE DIED. HE WAS BURIED WITH HIS GUN AND TOMAHAWK ATOP SAGAMORE HILL, ONE OF THE HIGHEST AND MOST SIGNIFICANT HILLS IN THE AREA.

A FEW YEARS LATER, HIS REMAINS WERE DISTURBED BY A GROUP OF IPSWICH YOUTHS WHO WERE IMMEDIATELY ARRESTED, REPRIMANDED AND MADE TO DO PENANCE. THE BONES WERE RETURNED TO THE HILLTOP GRAVESITE . . . IN 1971, A MEMORIAL SERVICE . . . WAS HELD AND A LARGER STONE MONUMENT WAS ERECTED, BUT NOT UNTIL NOVEMBER 1993 WAS THE GRAVESITE CONSECRATED BY BOTH CHRISTIAN AND NATIVE AMERICAN RITUALS . . .

IN THE TRADITIONAL WAY OF THEIR PEOPLE, OEE-TASH, CHIEF OF THE PONKAPOAG PEOPLE OF THE MASSACHUSETTS NATION, PERFORMED THE SACRED CEREMONY AMIDST A TREMENDOUS FEELING OF EXPECTANCY AND THANKFULNESS ON SATURDAY, NOVEMBER 6, 1993.

—Text from an adjacent marker entitled "A Brief History of the Agawams and Masconomet," installed by the Town of Hamilton in 2009

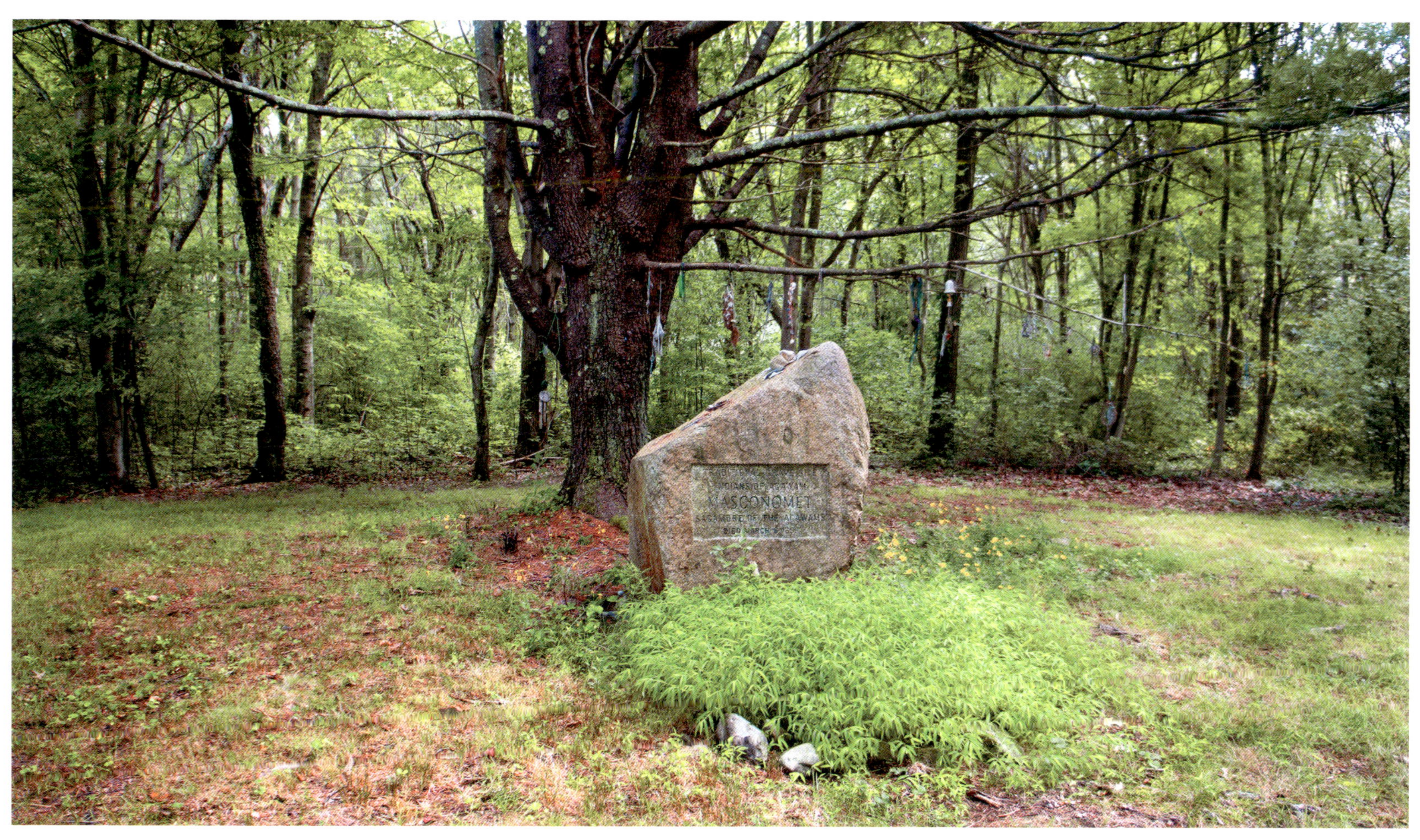

On Agawam/Pentucket/Pawtucket homelands. Gravesite of Masconomet, Sagamore of the Agawams. Hamilton, 2019.

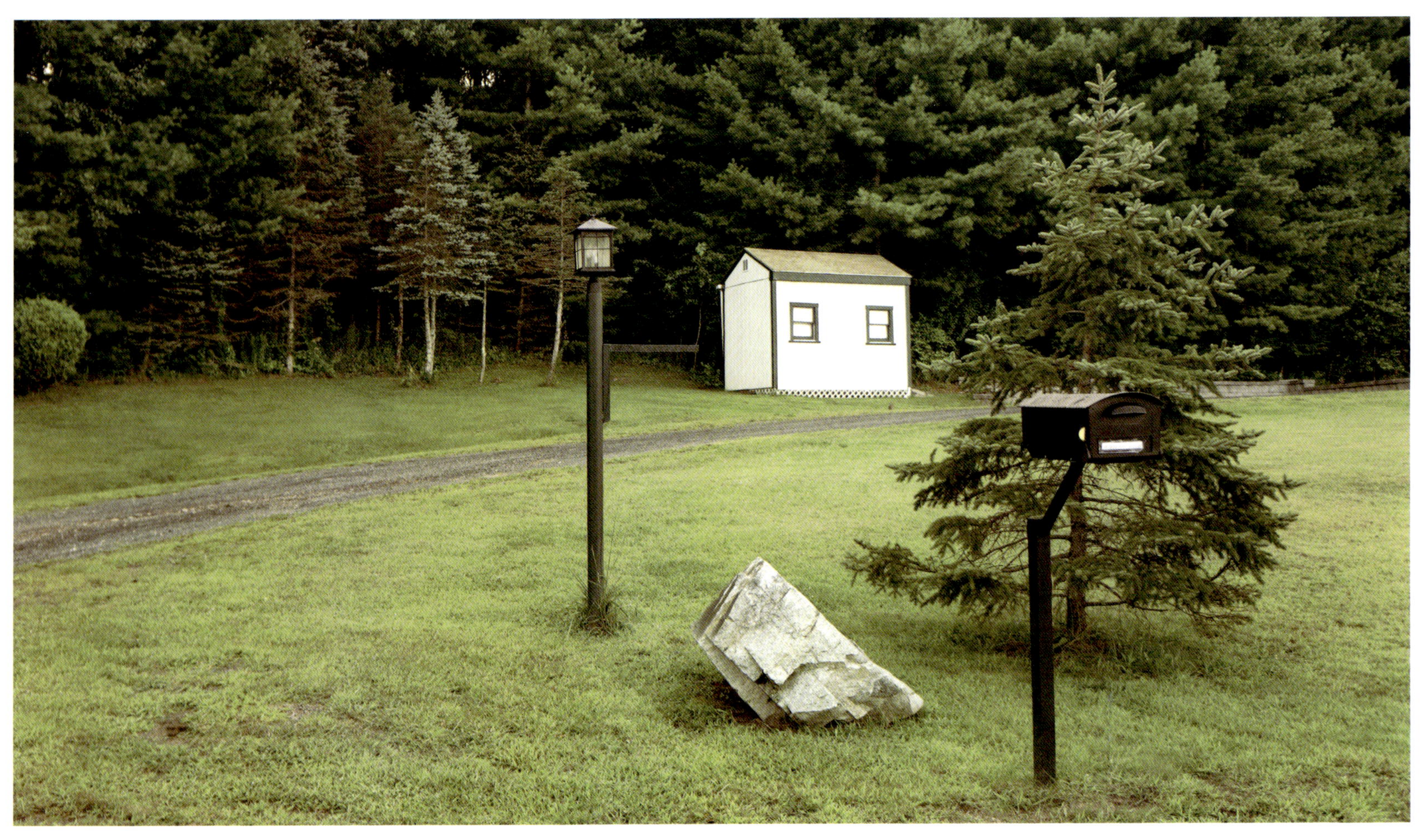

On Nipmuc and Pocumtuck homelands. Hatfield/Capawonk, 2015.

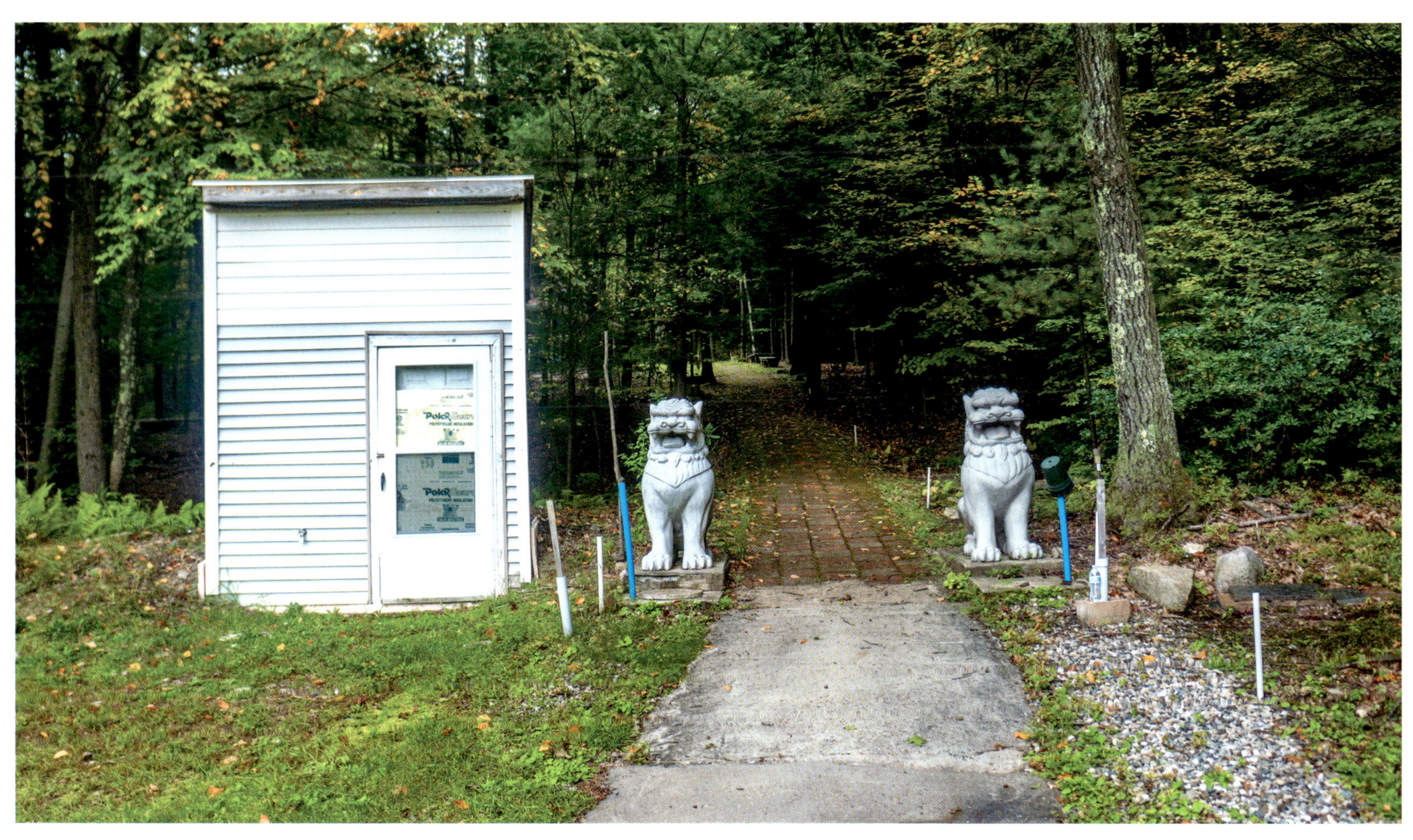

On Nipmuc and Pocumtuck homelands. Leverett, 2018.

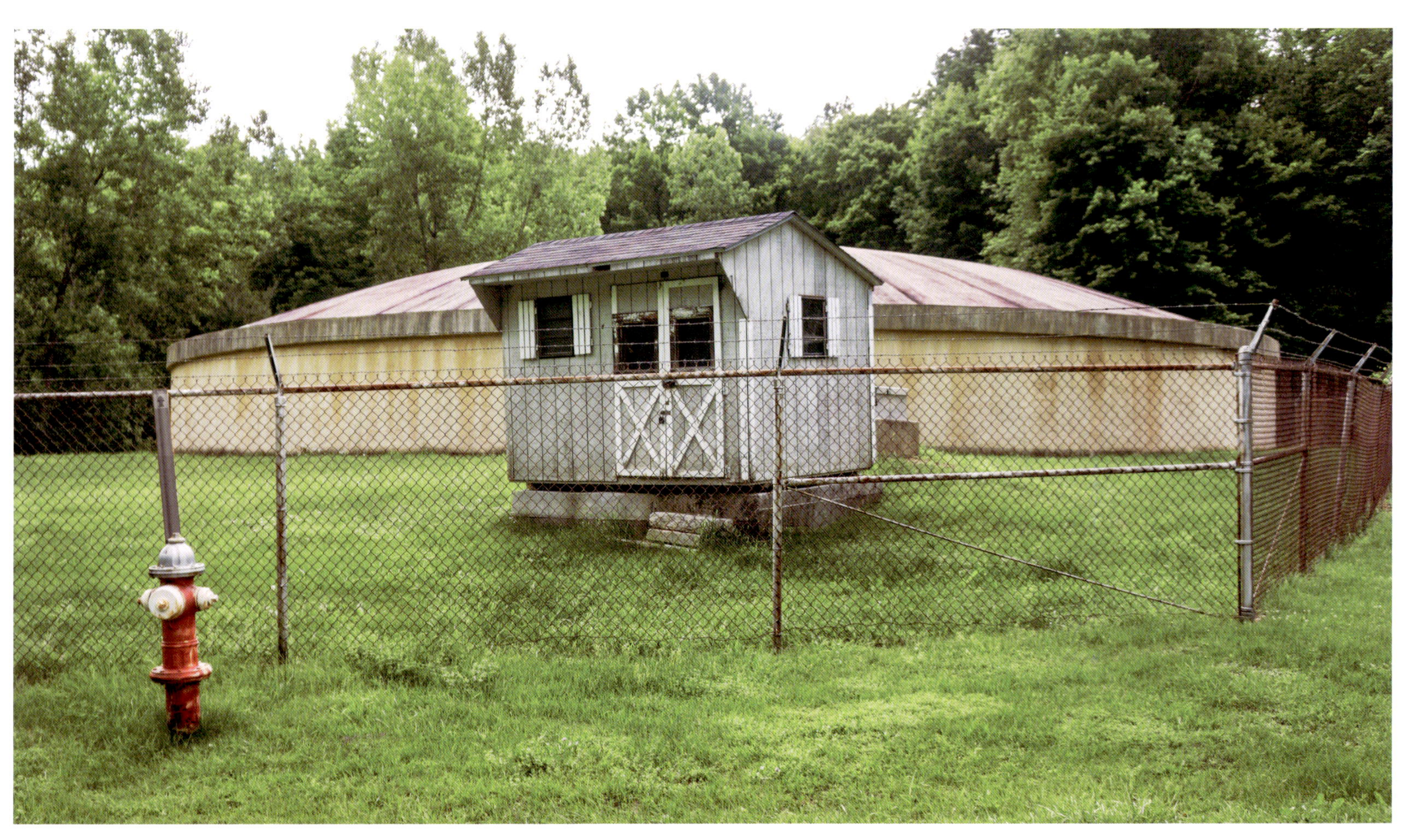

On Mohican homelands. Water tank. Adams, 2017.

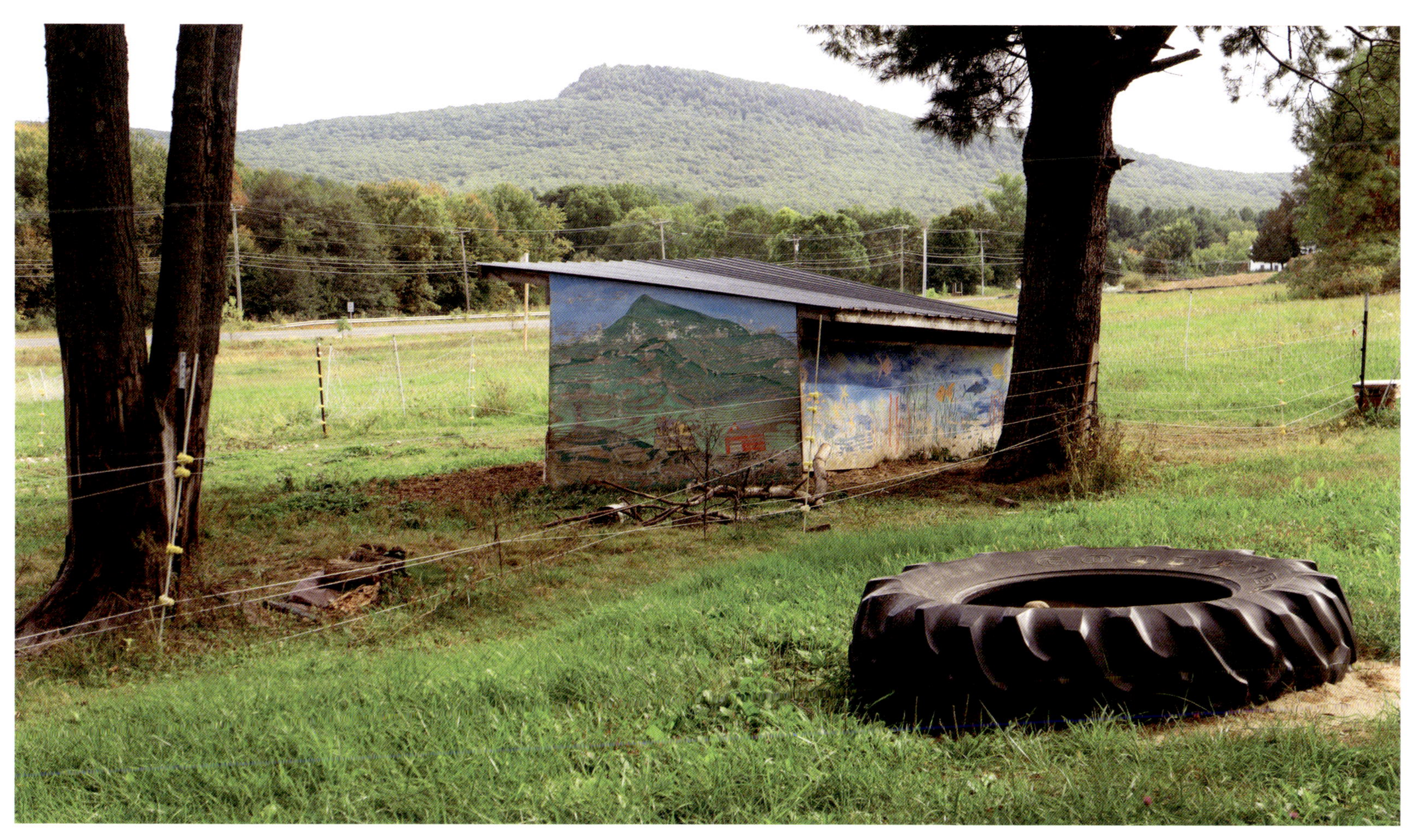

On Nipmuc and Pocumtuck homelands. Mount Norwottuck. Amherst, 2015.

17TH CENTURY PALISADE

IN 1676 THIS COMMON AND MOST OF ITS BUILDINGS WERE SURROUNDED BY A PALISADE BUILT OF SPLIT LOGS AT LEAST 3 FINGERS THICK AND 8 FEET HIGH. THIS FORTIFICATION WAS ONE MILE LONG BY FORTY RODS WIDE. HADLEY WAS THEN A FRONTIER OUTPOST WHICH FELT THREATENED BY NATIVE AMERICAN ATTACK.

—Marker installed by the Hadley Historical Commission in 1995

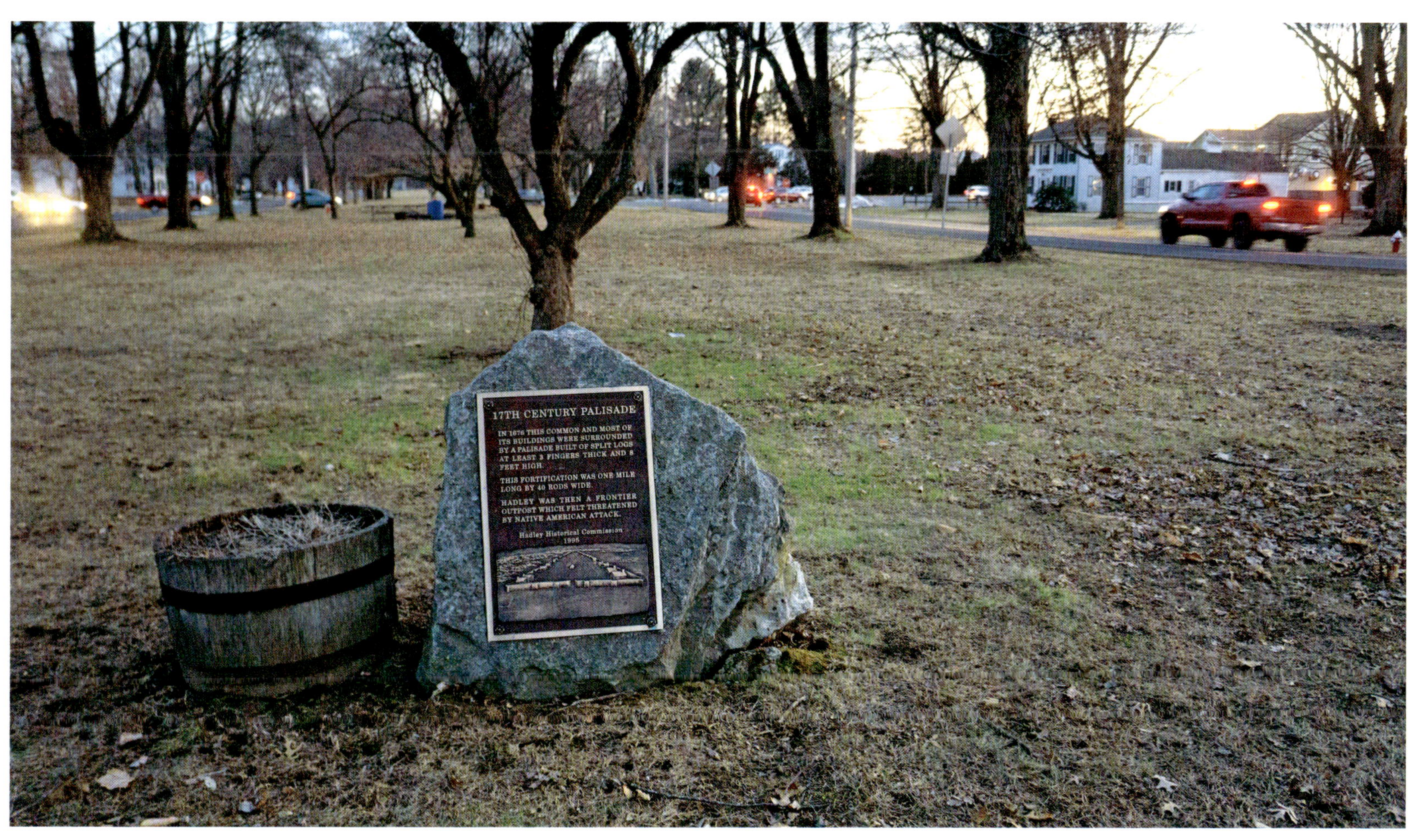

On Nipmuc and Pocumtuck homelands. Hadley, also known as Norwottuck, 2020.

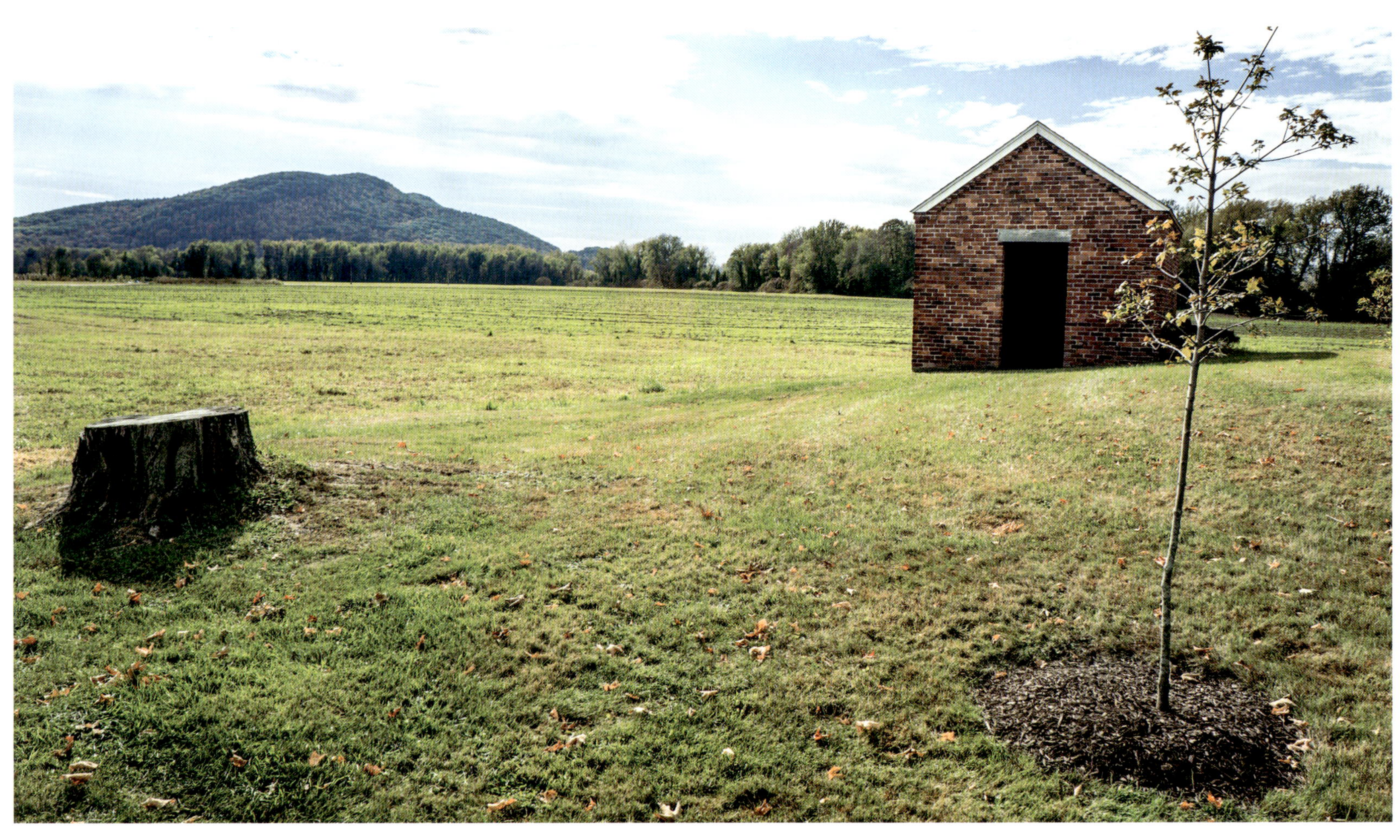

On Nipmuc and Pocumtuck homelands. Hadley/Norwottuck, 2017.

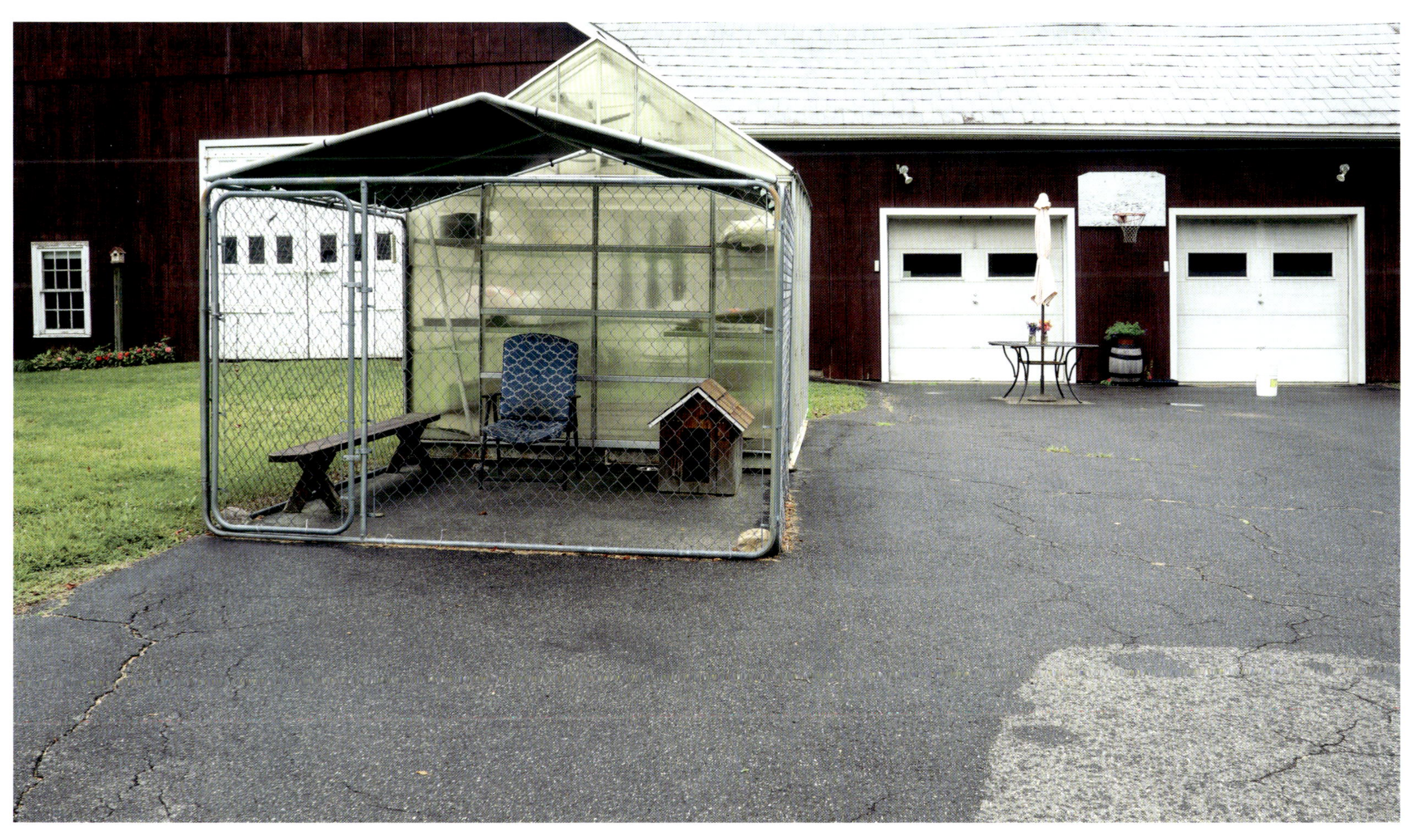

On Nipmuc and Pocumtuck homelands. Hadley/Norwottuck, 2019.

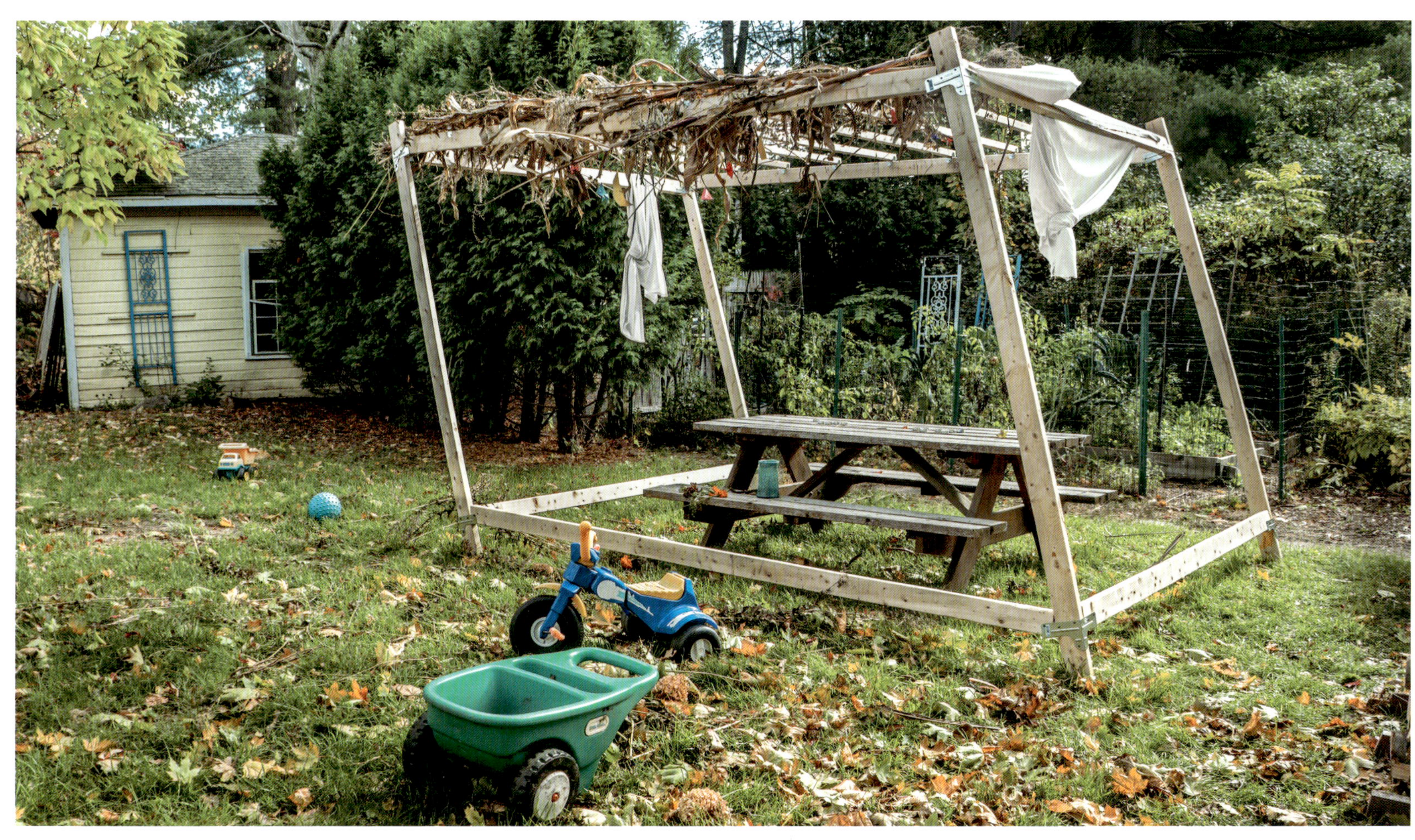

On Nipmuc and Pocumtuck homelands. Northampton/Nonotuck, 2017.

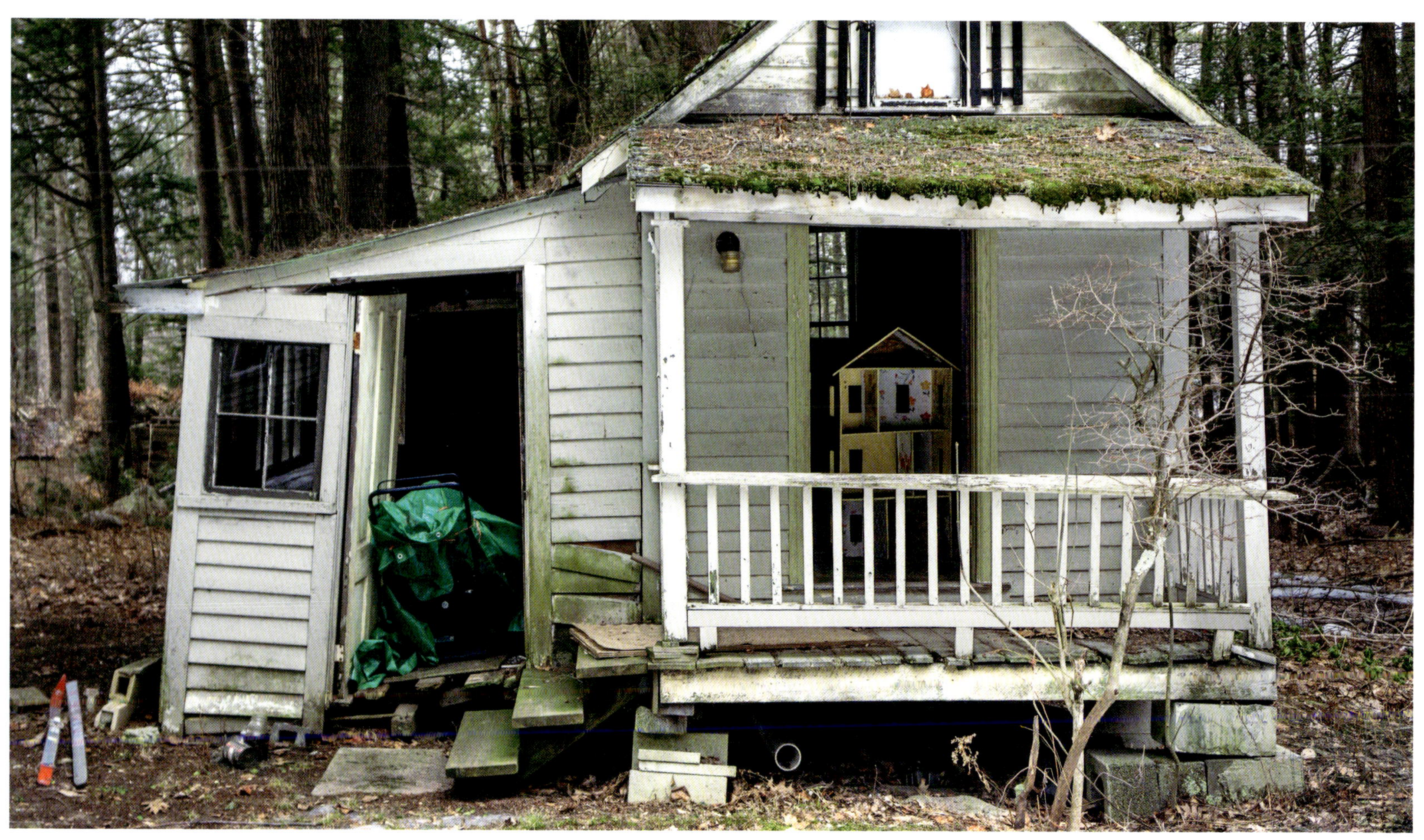

On Nipmuc and Pocumtuck homelands. Northampton/Nonotuck, 2016.

HATFIELD

BEFORE 1870 PART OF HADLEY.
THRICE ATTACKED BY INDIANS
DURING KING PHILIP'S WAR.

—Marker installed by the Massachusetts Bay Colony Tercentenary Commission in 1930

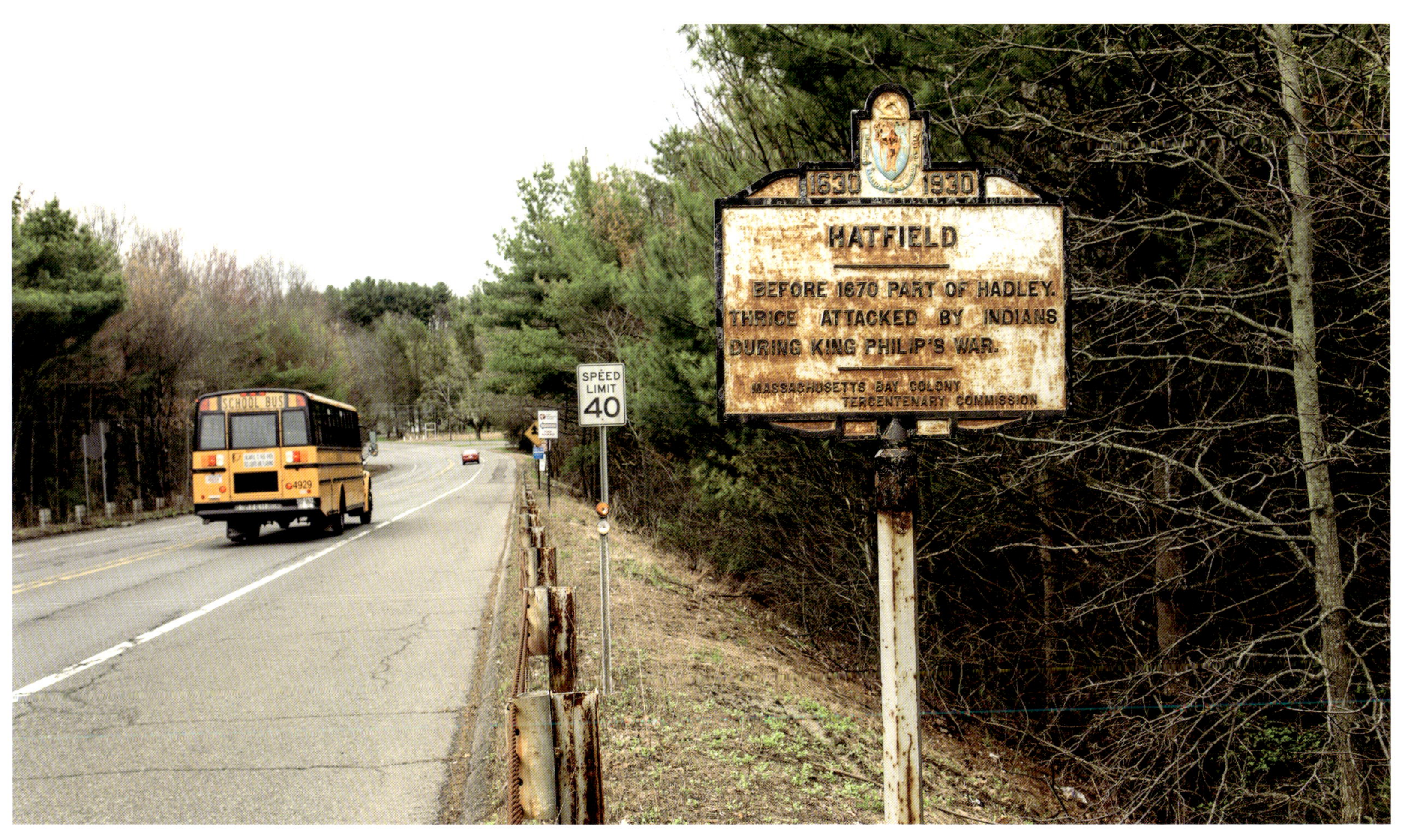

On Nipmuc and Pocumtuck homelands. Hatfield/Capawonk, 2019.

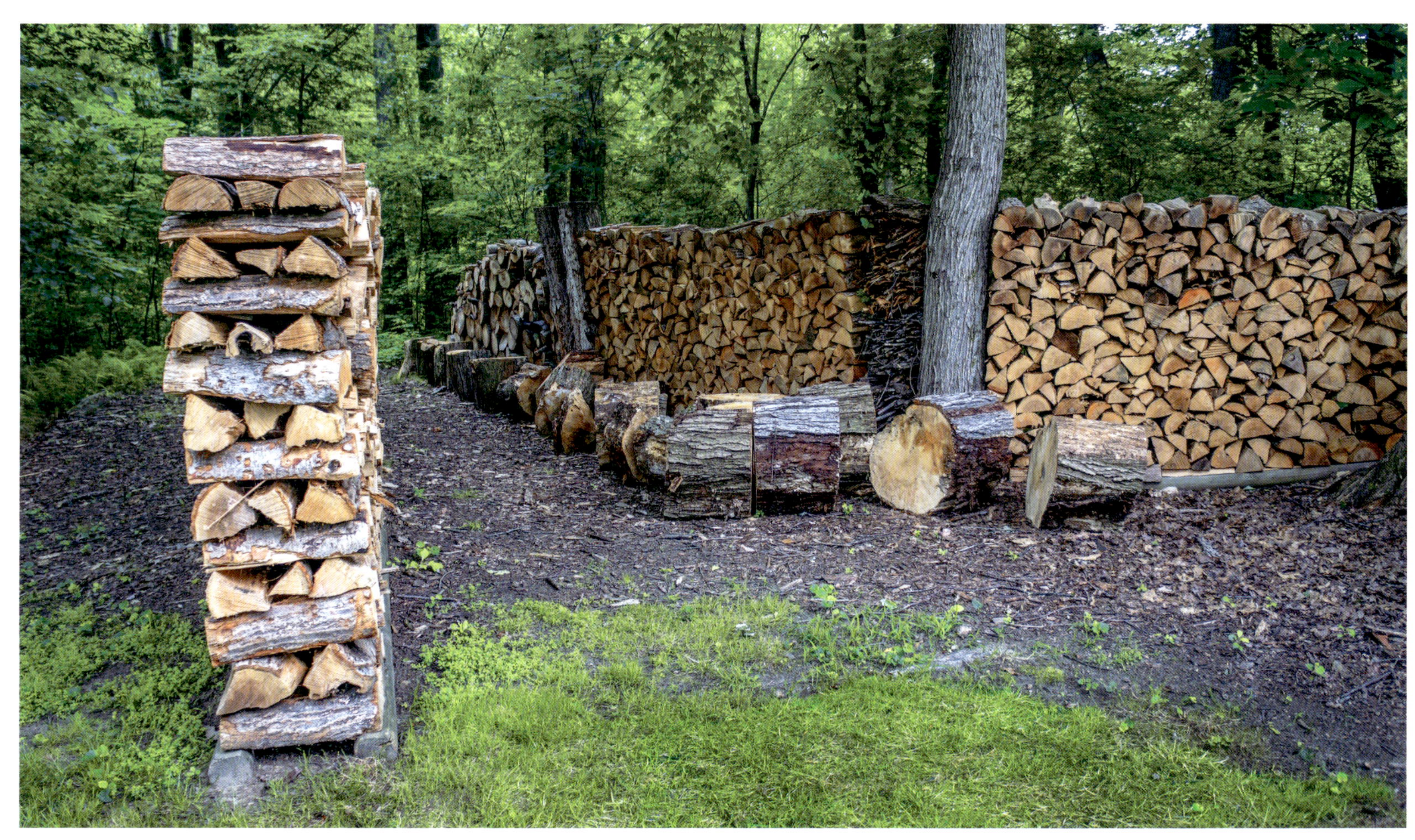

On Nipmuc and Pocumtuck homelands. Hatfield/Capawonk, 2020.

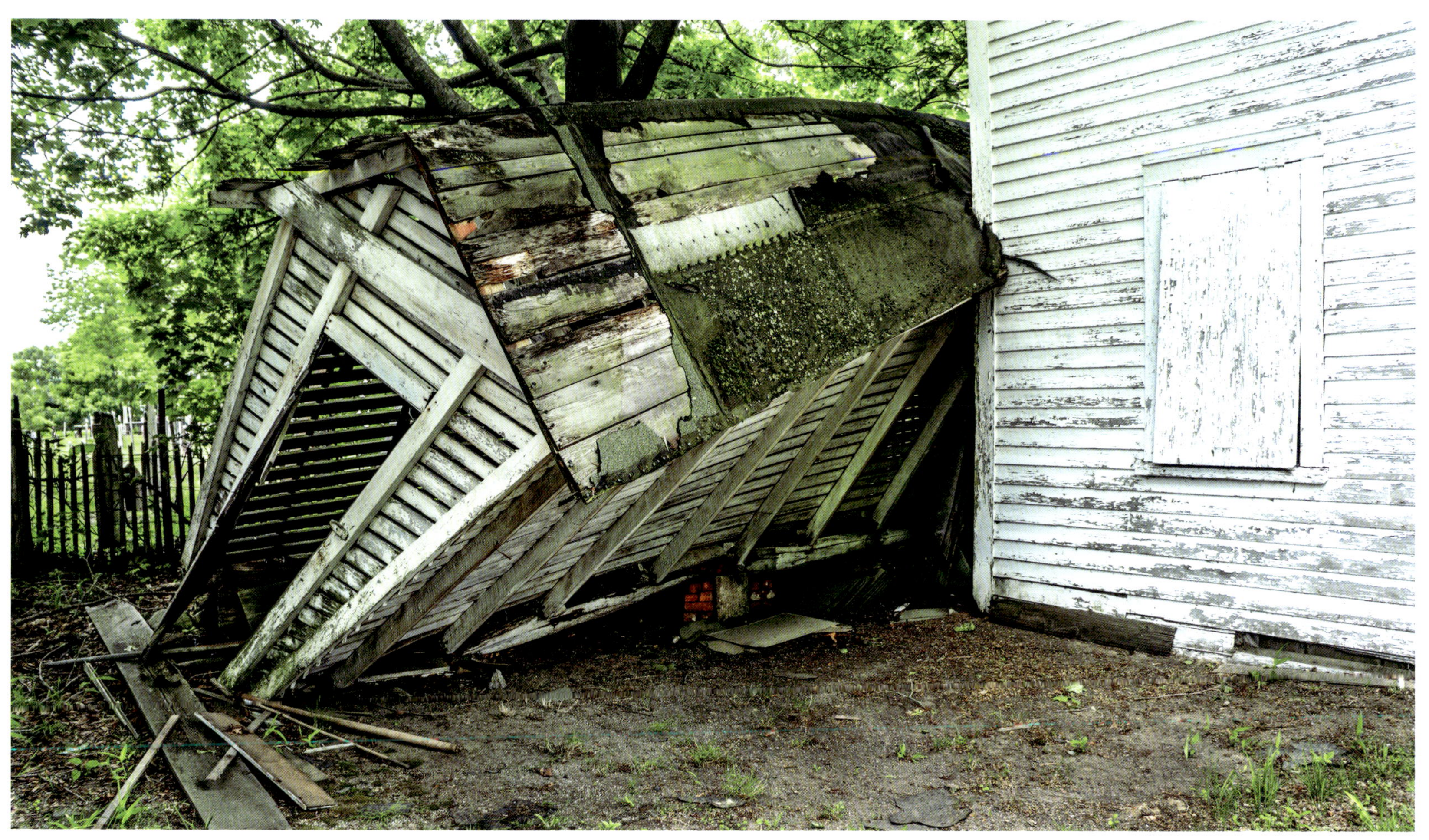

On Nipmuc and Pocumtuck homelands. Corn crib. Hatfield/Capawonk, 2020.

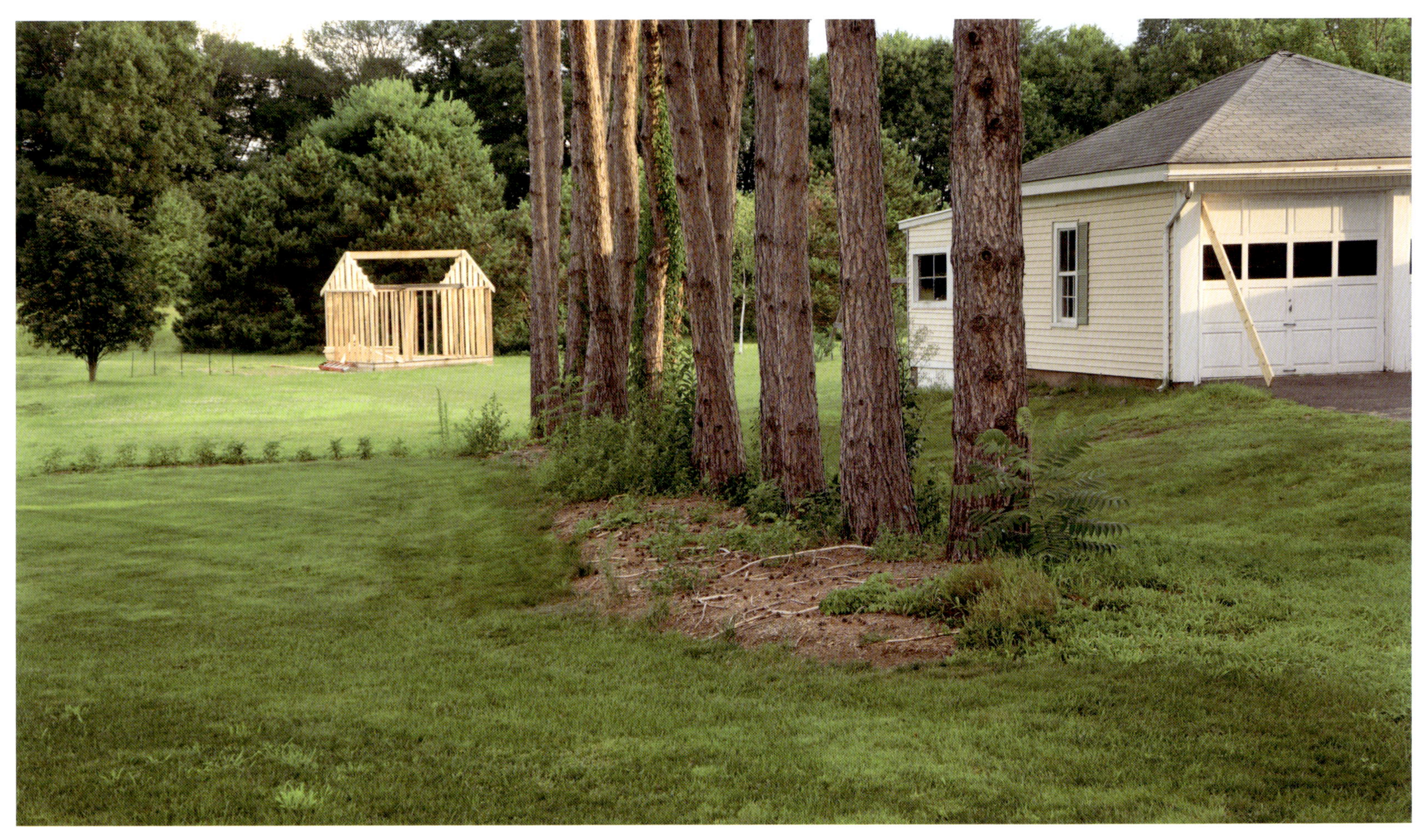

On Nipmuc and Pocumtuck homelands. Hatfield/Capawonk, 2015.

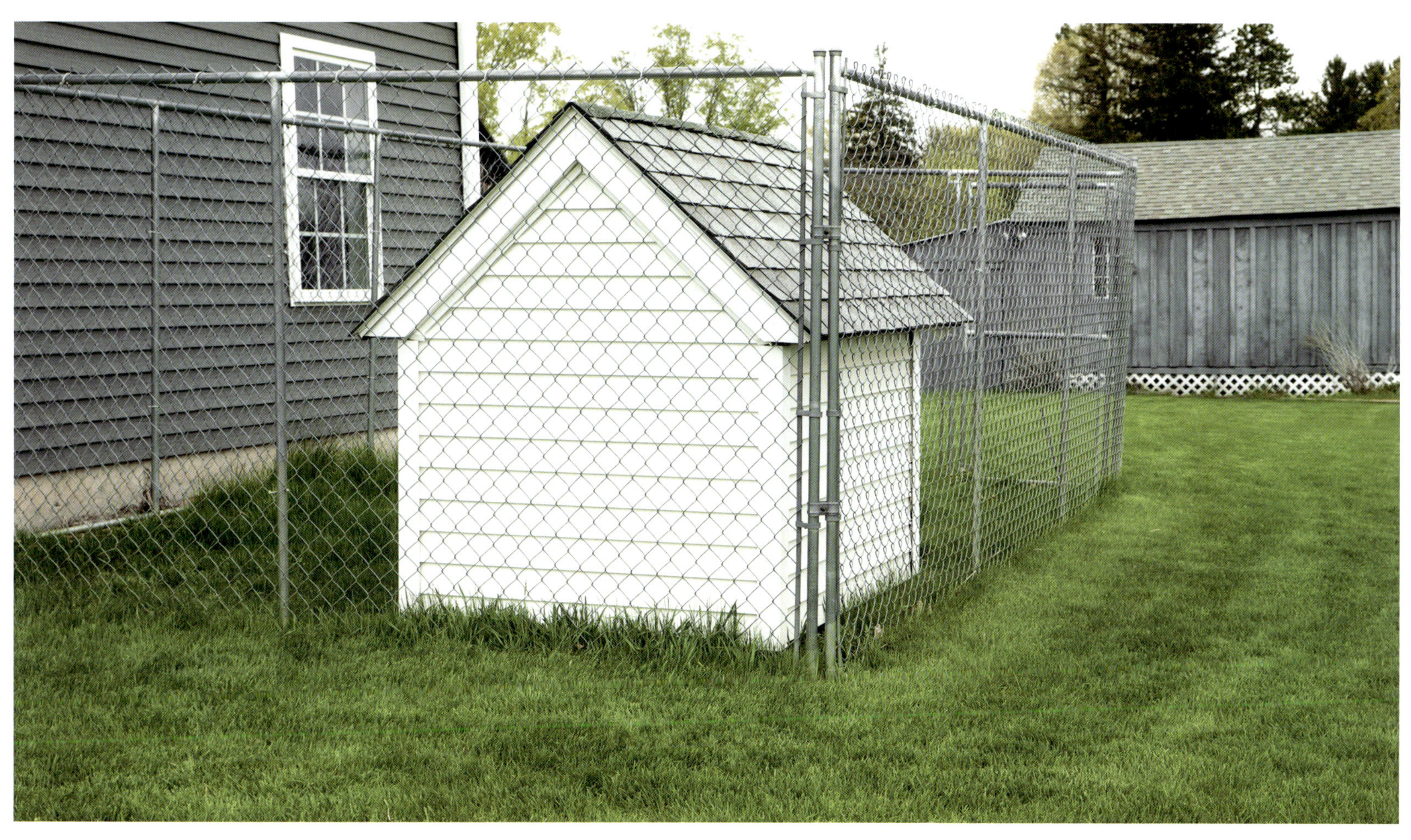

On Nipmuc and Pocumtuck homelands. Hatfield/Capawonk, 2016.

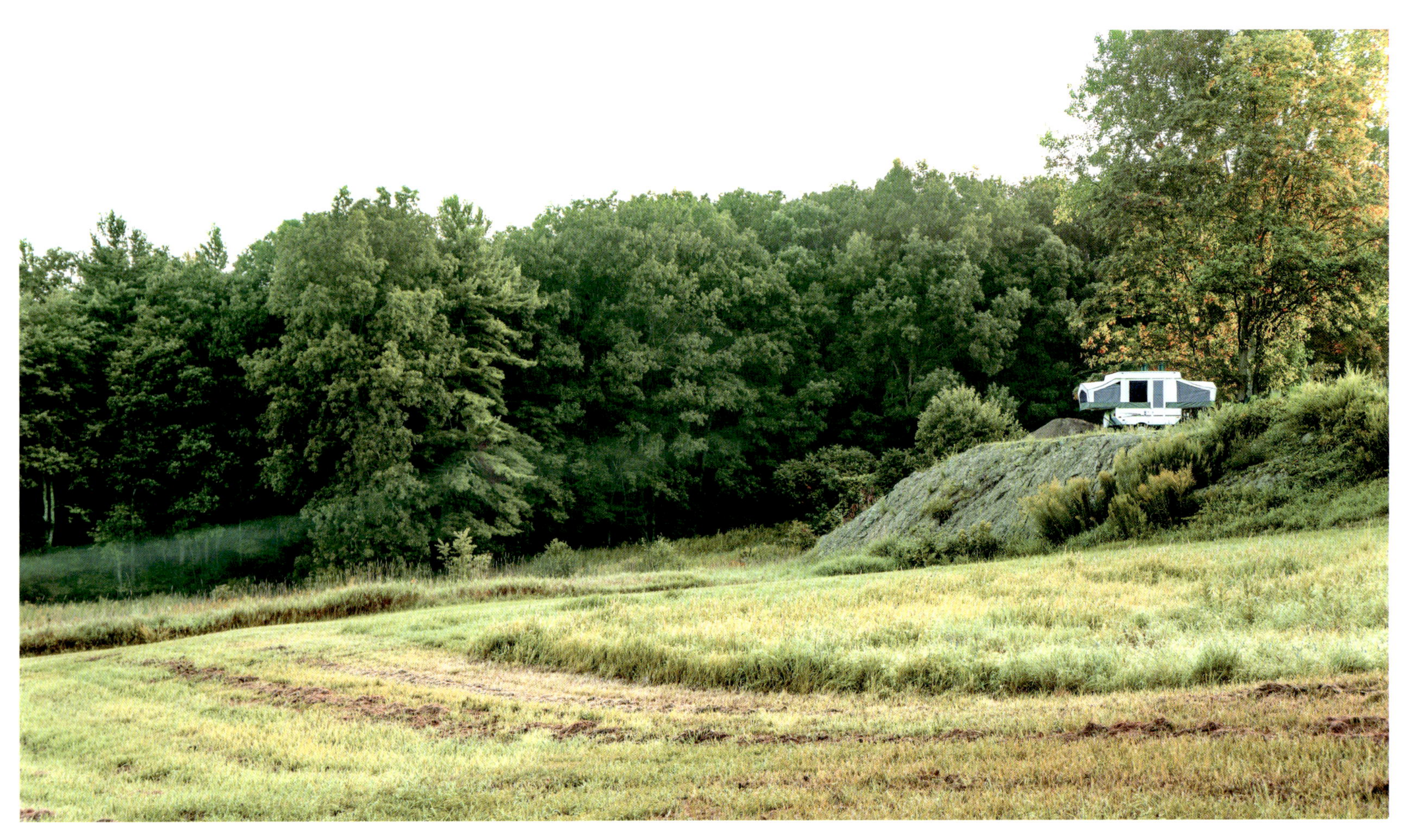

On Nipmuc and Pocumtuck homelands. Hatfield/Capawonk, 2015.

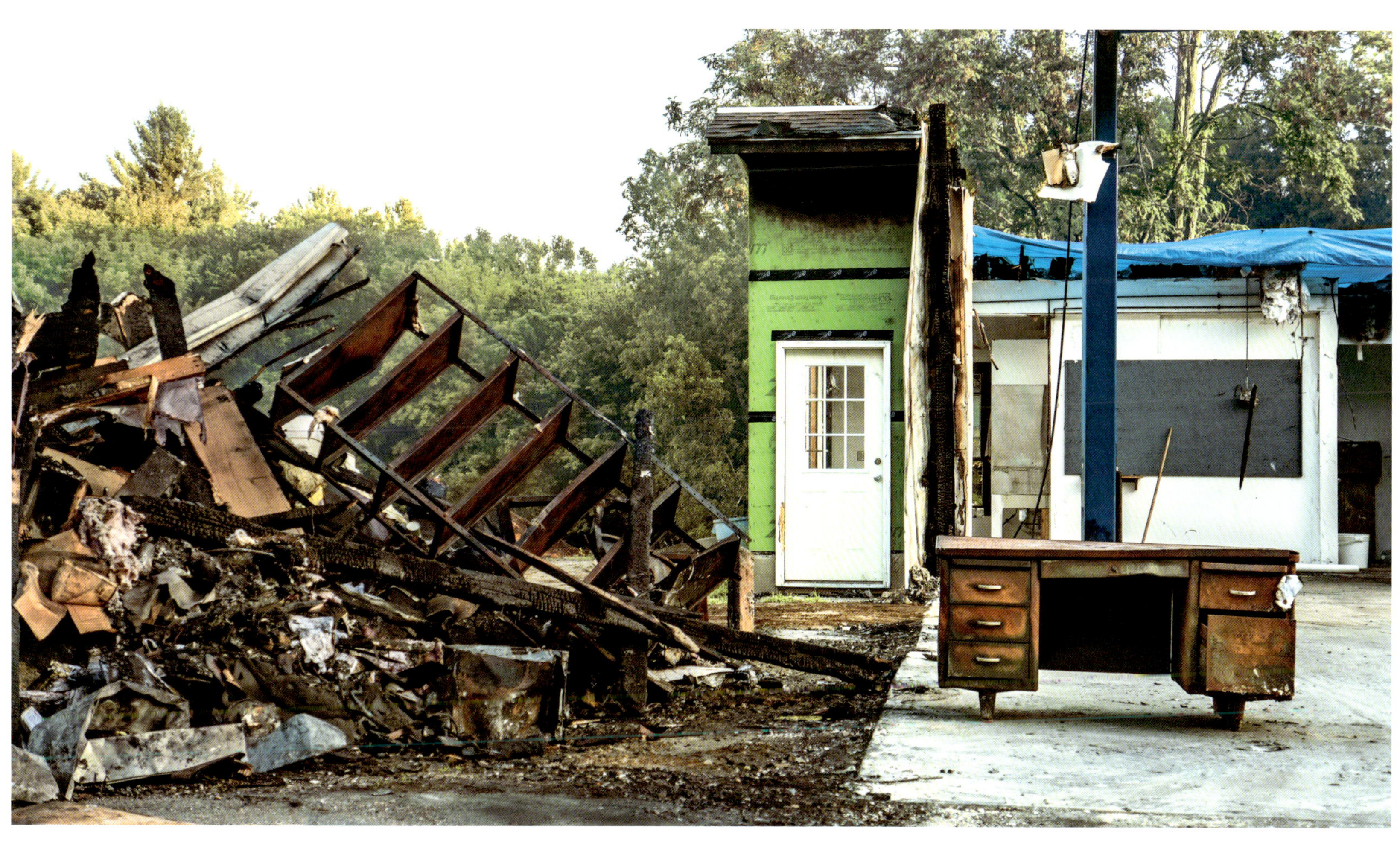

On Nipmuc and Pocumtuck homelands. Hatfield/Capawonk, 2015.

KING PHILIP'S HILL OFFERED EXCELLENT VIEWS NORTH AND SOUTH ALONG THE RIVER AND MAY HAVE BEEN USED AS A LOOK-OUT. SEVERAL CENTURIES AGO VEGETATION WOULD HAVE BEEN QUITE DIFFERENT WITH VERY LITTLE UNDERGROWTH BENEATH TALL, OLD-GROWTH TREES AND A DENSE LEAFY CANOPY. IT IS ALSO LIKELY THAT SCOUTS CLIMBED THE LARGE TREES TO WATCH FOR APPROACHING TRADERS OR INVADERS.

—Sign installed in 2008 by the Greater Northfield Watershed Association

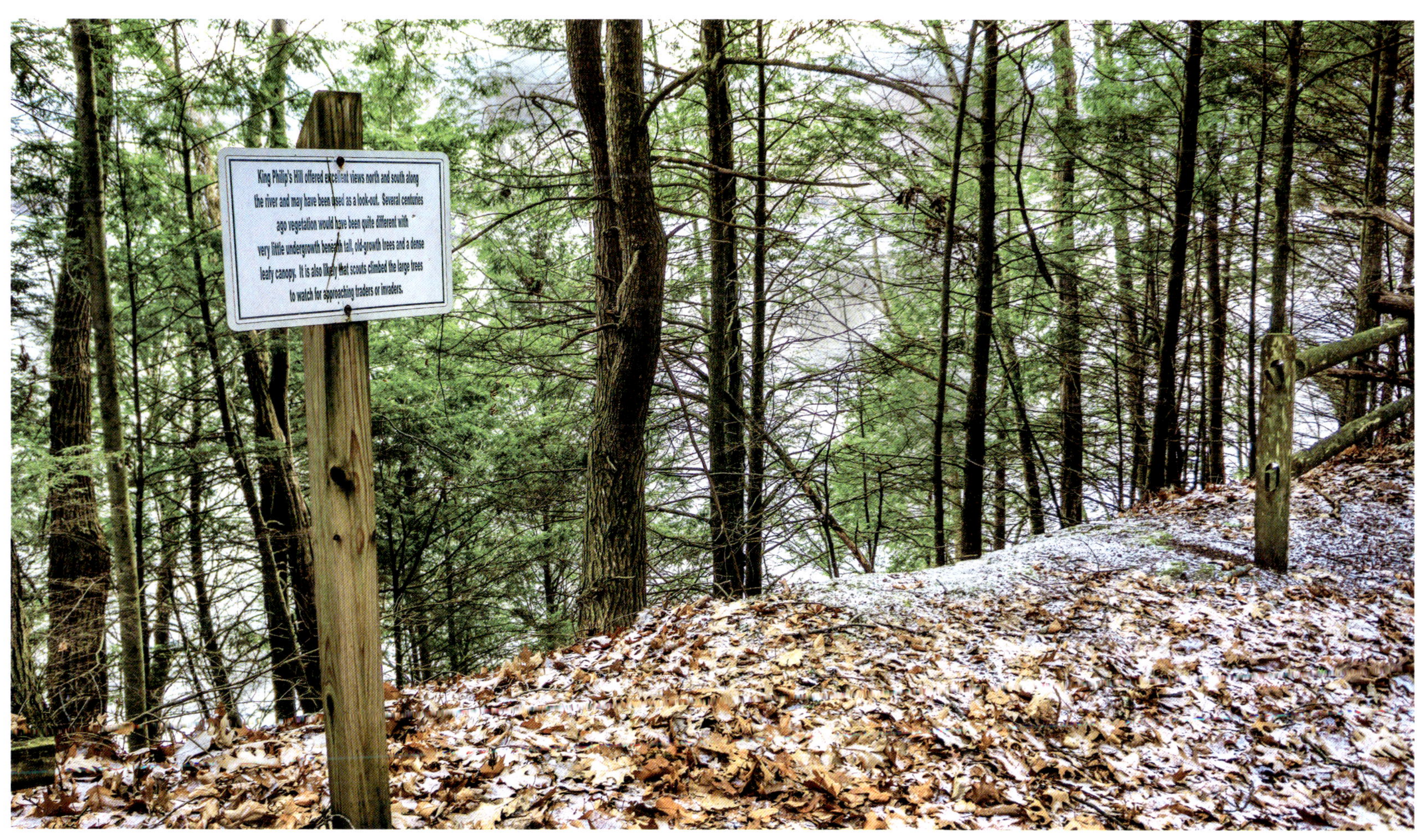

On Sokoki Abenaki homelands. Northfield, also known as Sokwakik, 2021.

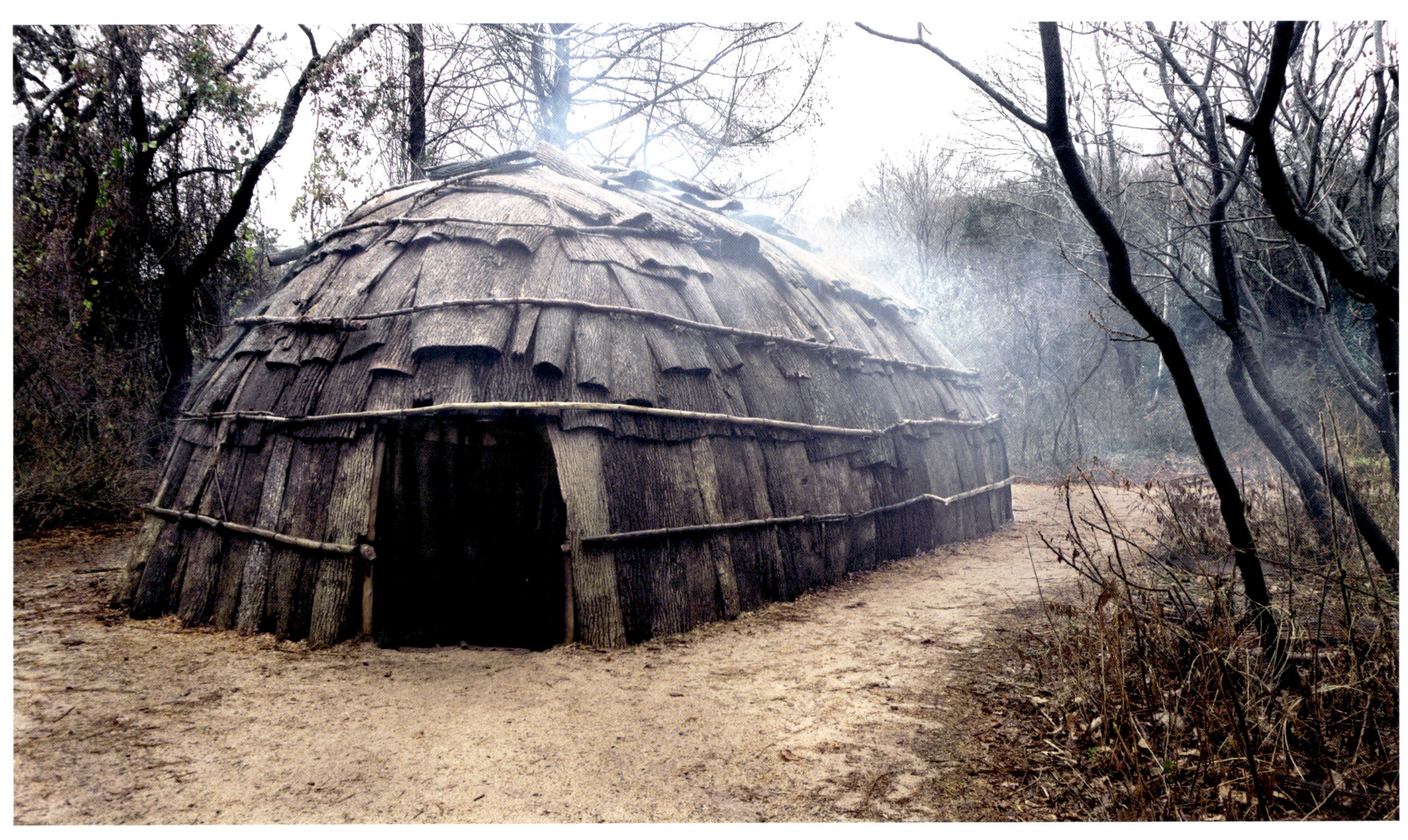

On Wampanoag and Massachusett homelands. A reconstructed *wetu* at Plimoth Patuxet Museums. Plymouth, also known as Patuxet, 2019.

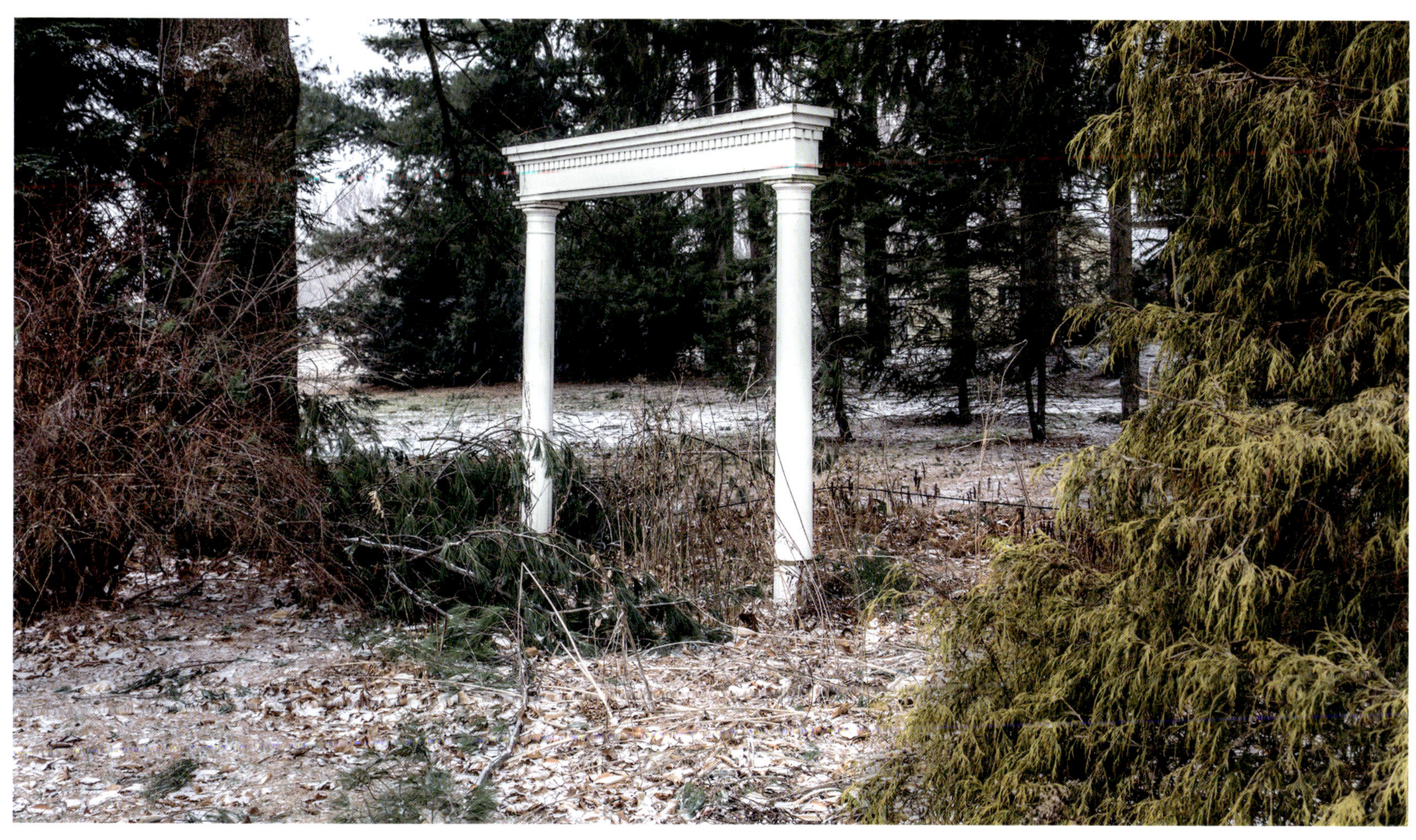

On Nipmuc and Pocumtuck homelands. Hadley/Norwottuck, 2016.

CAPTAIN WILLIAM TURNER
WITH 145 MEN SURPRISED AND
DESTROYED OVER 300 INDIANS
ENCAMPED AT THIS PLACE
MAY 19, 1676.

—Marker installed by the Pocumtuck Valley Memorial Association in 1900

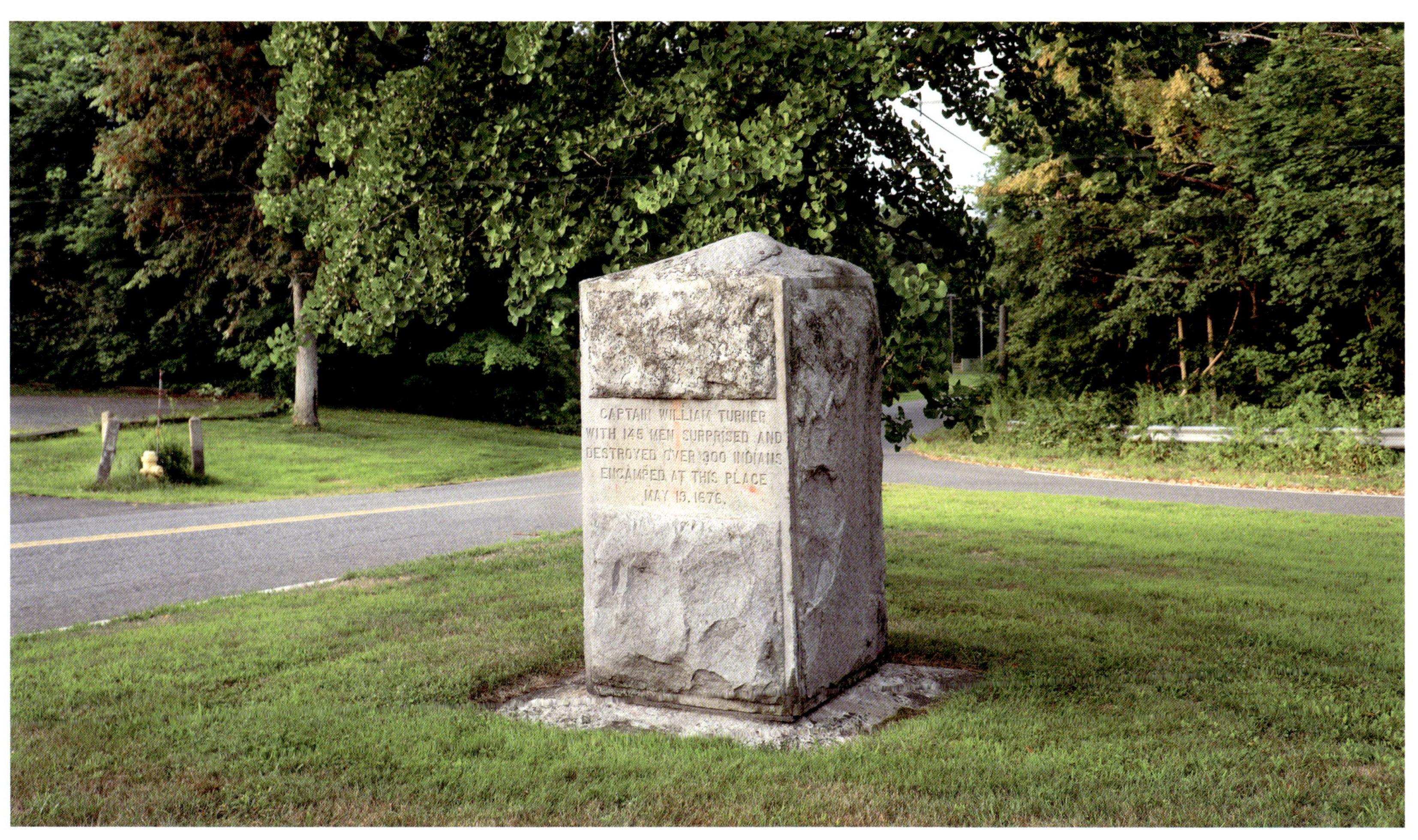

On Pennacook Abenaki homelands. Gill, also known as Peskeompskut, 2019.

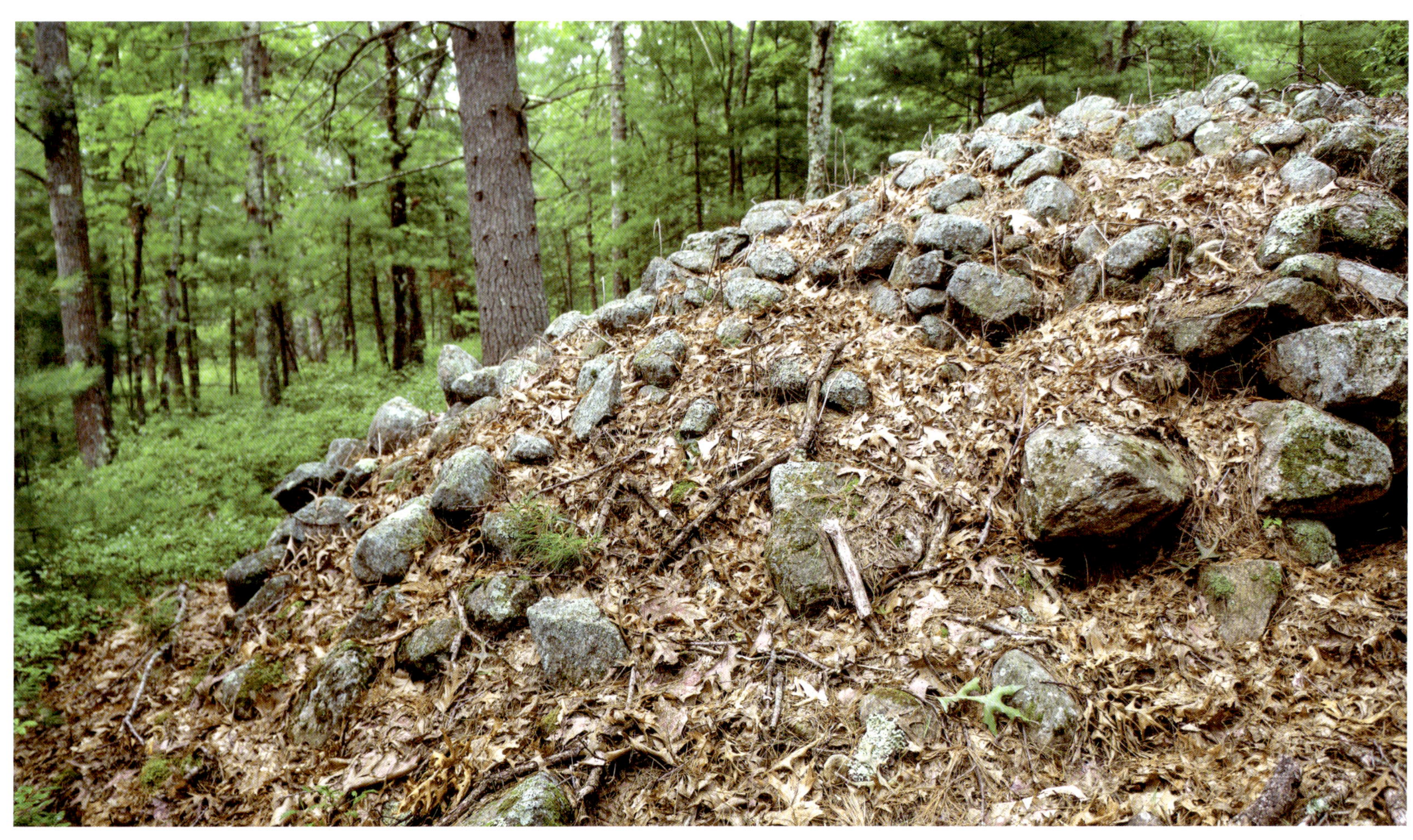

On Nipmuc homelands. Indigenous ceremonial stones on state forest land, date unknown. 2020.

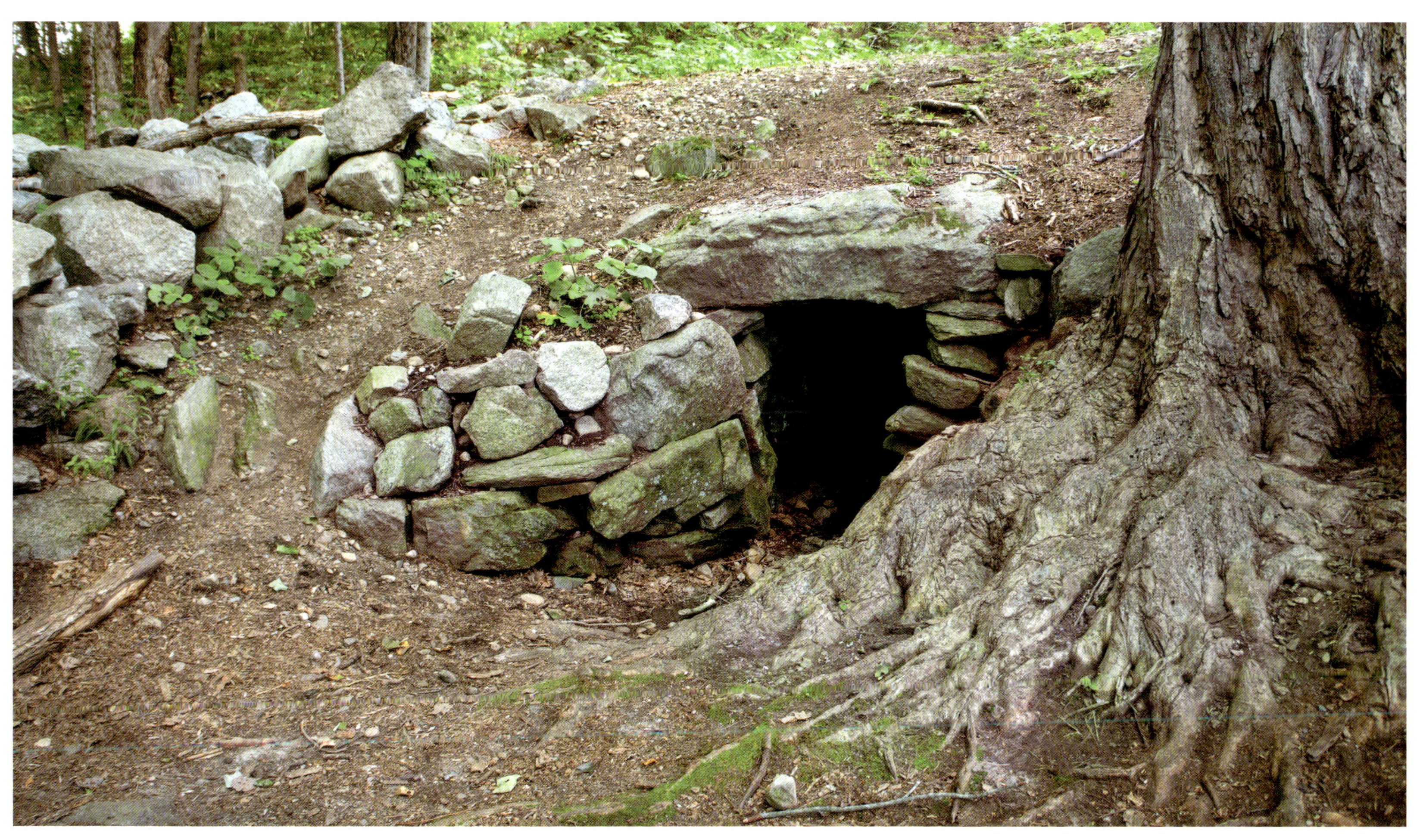

On Nipmuc homelands. Entrance to a spherical chamber, built between 1300 and 1600 CE. Upton, 2019.

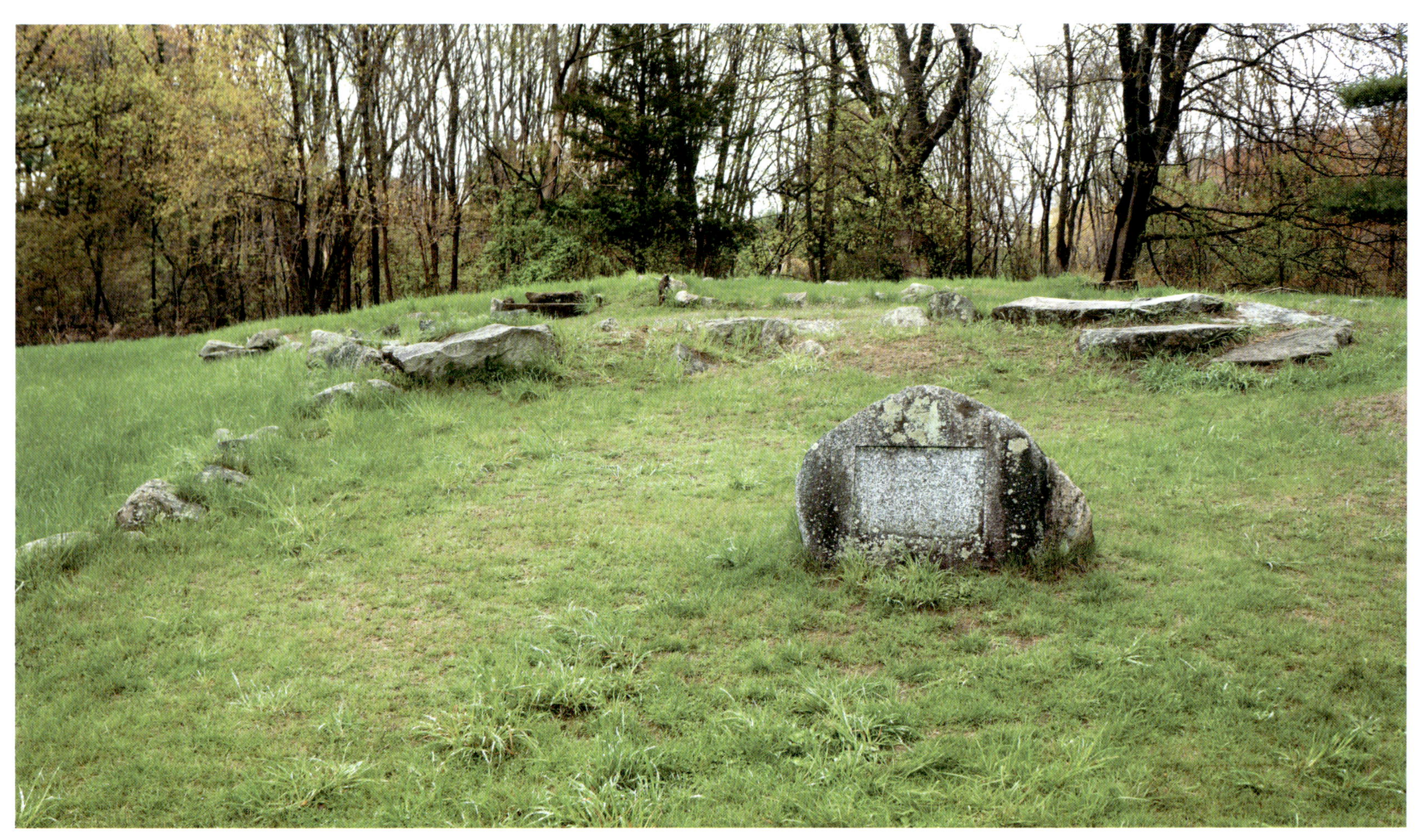

On Pawtucket and Massachusett homelands. Minuteman National Historic Park. Lexington, 2020.

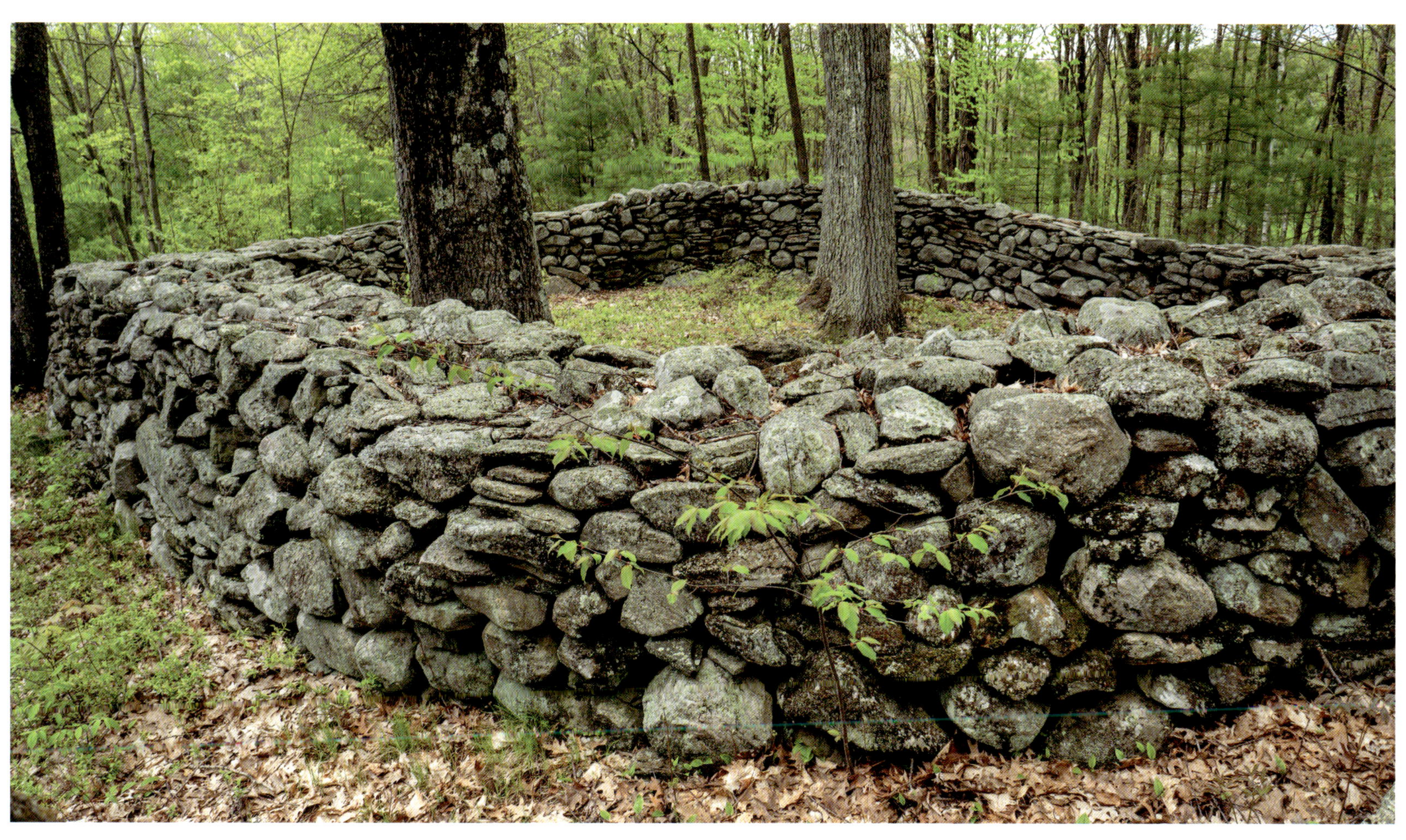

On Nipmuc and Pocumtuck homelands. A nineteenth-century pound. Shutesbury/Kingyiwngwalak, 2020.

METACOMET (KING PHILIP)

AFTER THE PILGRIMS' ARRIVAL, NATIVE AMERICANS IN NEW ENGLAND GREW INCREASINGLY FRUSTRATED WITH THE ENGLISH SETTLERS' ABUSE AND TREACHERY. METACOMET (KING PHILIP), A SON OF THE WAMPANOAG SACHEM KNOWN AS THE MASSASOIT (OUSAMEQUIN), CALLED UPON ALL NATIVE PEOPLE TO UNITE TO DEFEND THEIR HOMELANDS AGAINST ENCROACHMENT.

THE RESULTING 'KING PHILIP'S WAR' LASTED FROM 1675–1676. METACOMET WAS MURDERED IN RHODE ISLAND IN AUGUST 1676, AND HIS BODY WAS MUTILATED. HIS HEAD WAS IMPALED ON A PIKE AND WAS DISPLAYED NEAR THIS SITE FOR MORE THAN 20 YEARS. ONE HAND WAS SENT TO BOSTON, THE OTHER TO ENGLAND. METACOMET'S WIFE AND SON, ALONG WITH THE FAMILIES OF MANY OF THE NATIVE AMERICAN COMBATANTS, WERE SOLD INTO SLAVERY IN THE WEST INDIES BY THE ENGLISH VICTORS.

—Marker installed by the United American Indians of New England in 1998

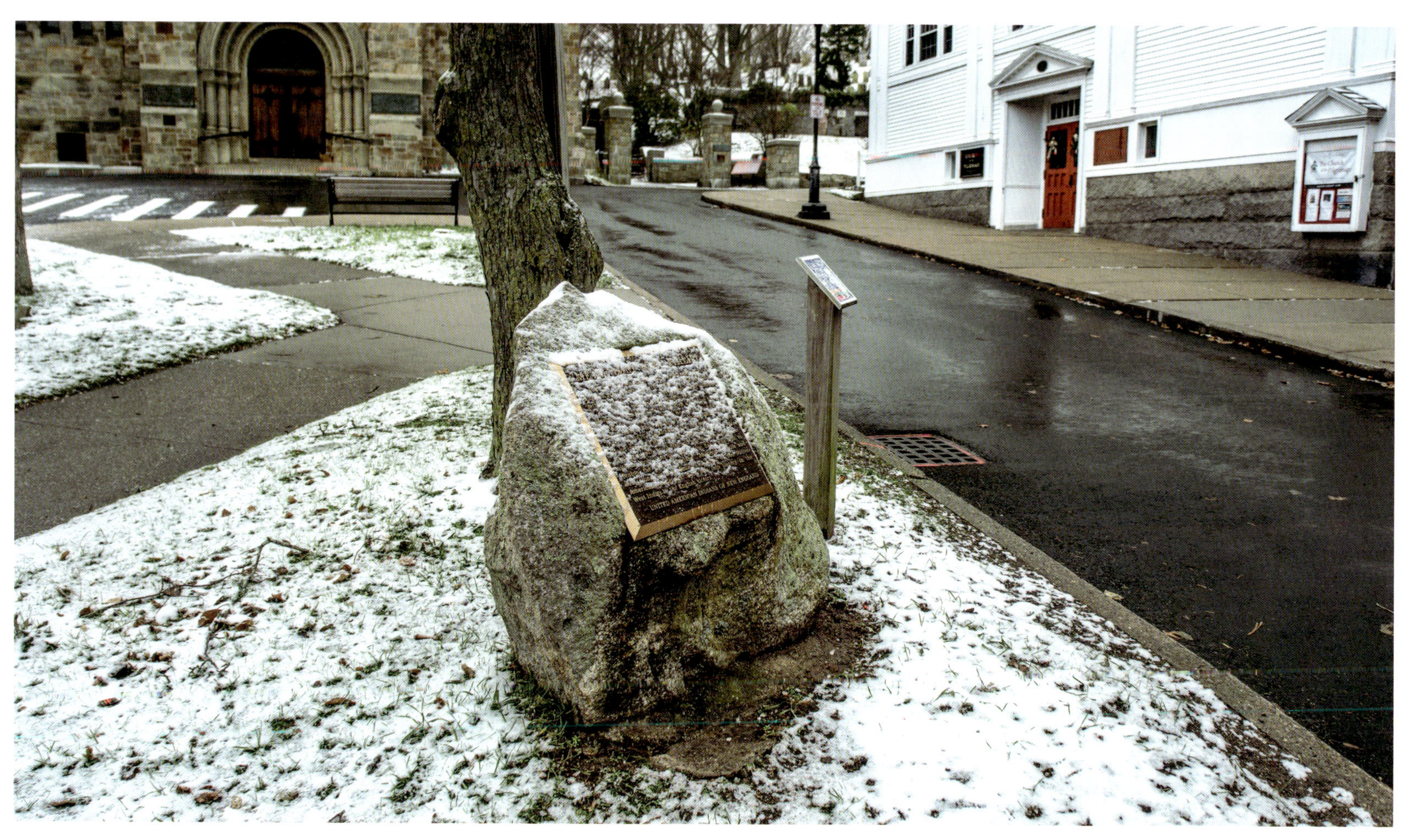

On Wampanoag homelands. Plymouth/Patuxet, 2020.

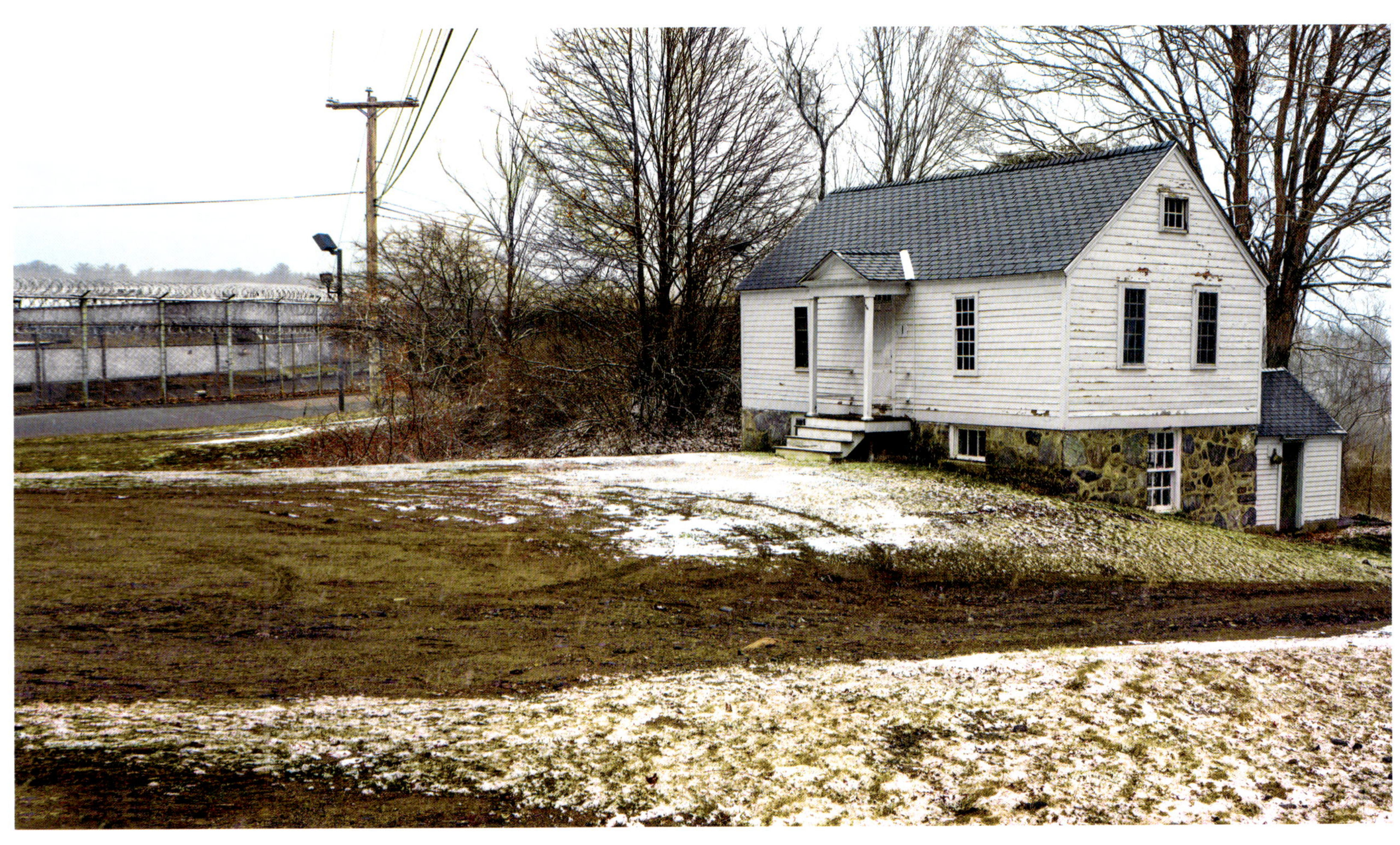

On Nipmuc and Pennacook Abenaki homelands. Shirley, 2018.

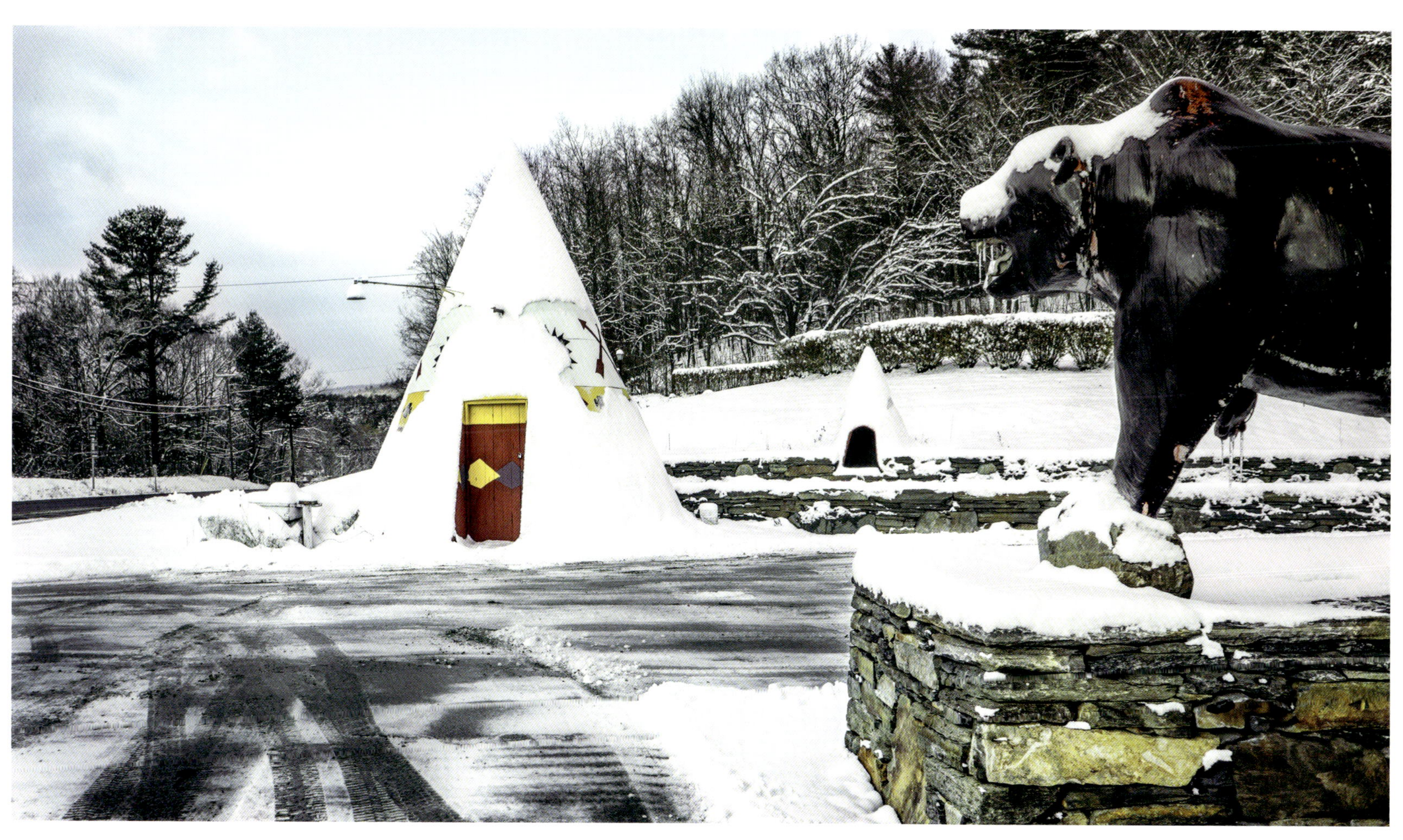

On Nipmuc and Pocumtuck homelands. Charlemont, 2017.

THIS MONUMENT STANDS UPON THE OLD MEETING HOUSE HILL, AND IS WITHIN THE LIMITS OF THE OLD FORT BUILT A.D. 1689 AND WHICH REMAINED UNTIL A.D. 1758 AND WAS ONE OF THE CHIEF DEFENSES OF THE EARLY SETTLERS AGAINST THE ATTACKS OF THE SAVAGE INDIANS . . .

—Civil War monument installed with private funds in 1867 and restored in 2019 with funds from the Deerfield Academy Class of 1969 as well as the Town of Deerfield and the Commonwealth of Massachusetts under the Community Preservation Act, in conjunction with the conservation efforts of the Pocumtuck Valley Memorial Association.

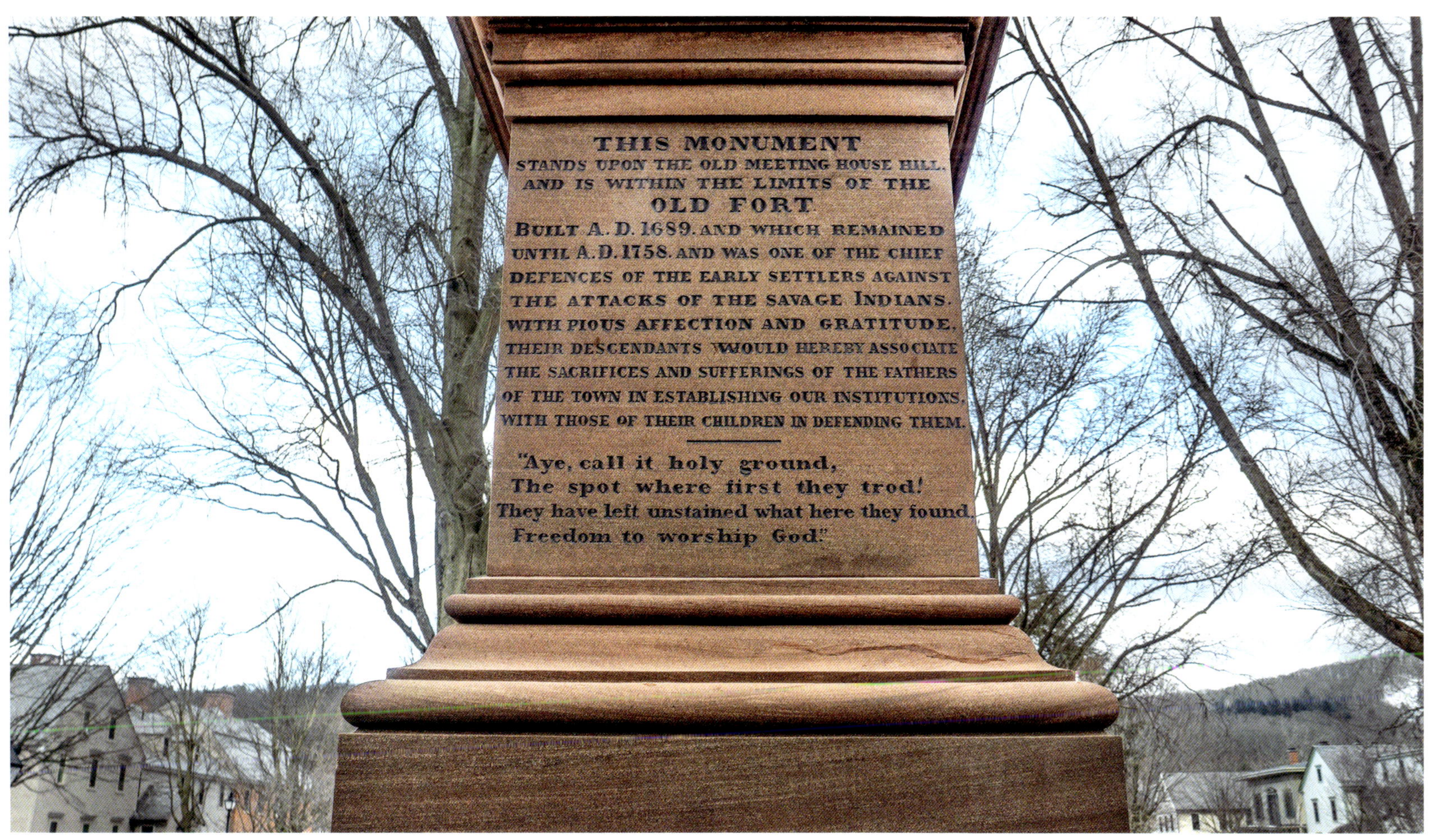

On Nipmuc and Pocumtuck homelands. Deerfield, also known as Pocumtuck, 2021.

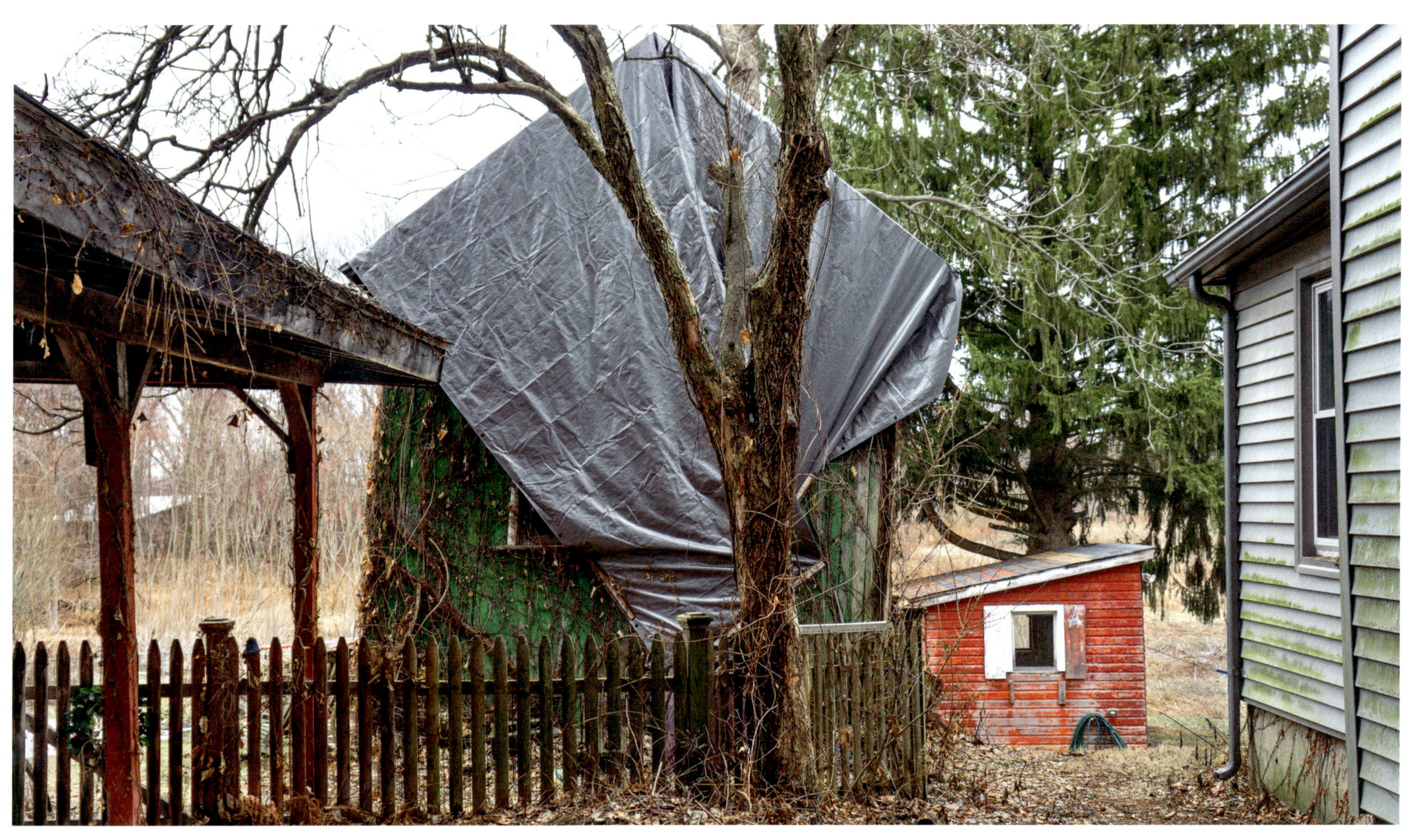

On Nipmuc and Pocumtuck homelands. Northampton/Nonotuck, 2017.

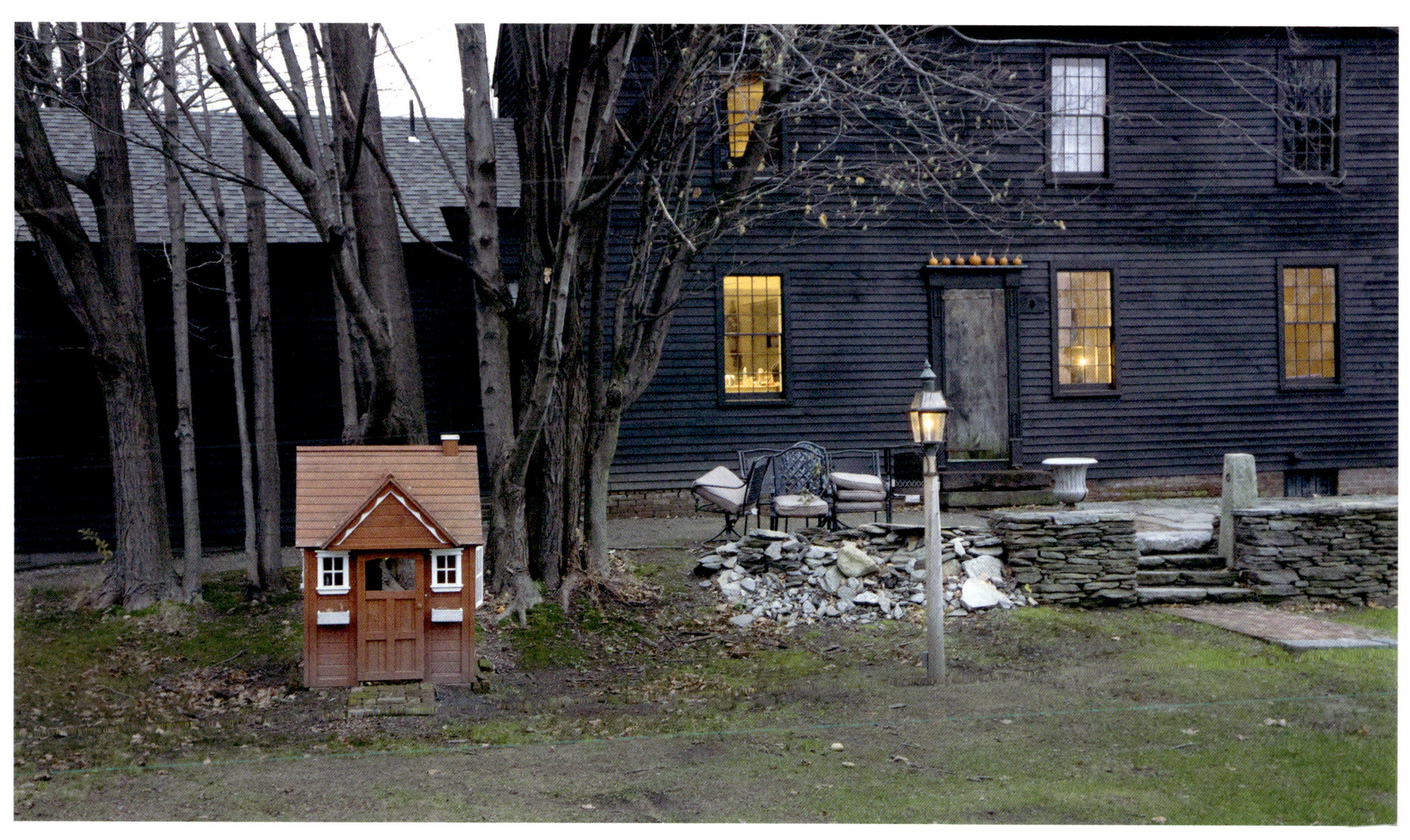

On Nipmuc and Pocumtuck homelands. Hatfield/Capawonk, 2015.

NATIONAL DAY OF MOURNING

SINCE 1970, NATIVE AMERICANS HAVE GATHERED AT NOON ON COLE'S HILL IN PLYMOUTH TO COMMEMORATE A NATIONAL DAY OF MOURNING ON THE U.S. THANKSGIVING HOLIDAY. MANY NATIVE AMERICANS DO NOT CELEBRATE THE ARRIVAL OF THE PILGRIMS AND OTHER EUROPEAN SETTLERS. TO THEM, THANKSGIVING IS A REMINDER OF THE GENOCIDE OF MILLIONS OF THEIR PEOPLE, THE THEFT OF THEIR LANDS, AND THE RELENTLESS ASSAULT ON THEIR CULTURE. PARTICIPANTS IN NATIONAL DAY OF MOURNING HONOR NATIVE ANCESTORS AND THE STRUGGLES OF NATIVE PEOPLES TO SURVIVE TODAY. IT IS A DAY OF REMEMBRANCE AND SPIRITUAL CONNECTION AS WELL AS A PROTEST OF THE RACISM AND OPPRESSION WHICH NATIVE AMERICANS CONTINUE TO EXPERIENCE.

—Marker installed by the Town of Plymouth on behalf of the United American Indians of New England in 1998

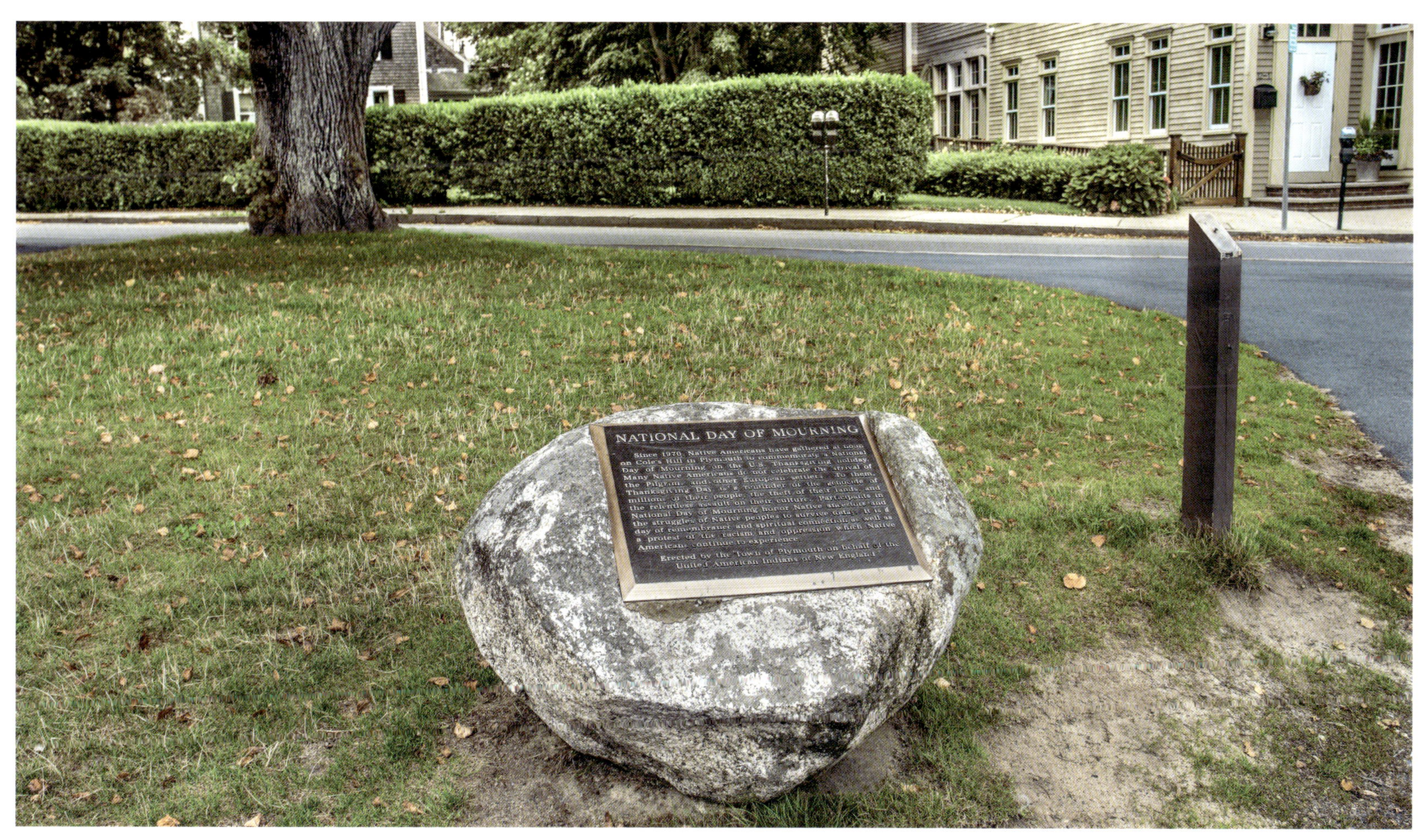

On Wampanoag homelands. Plymouth/Patuxet, 2019.

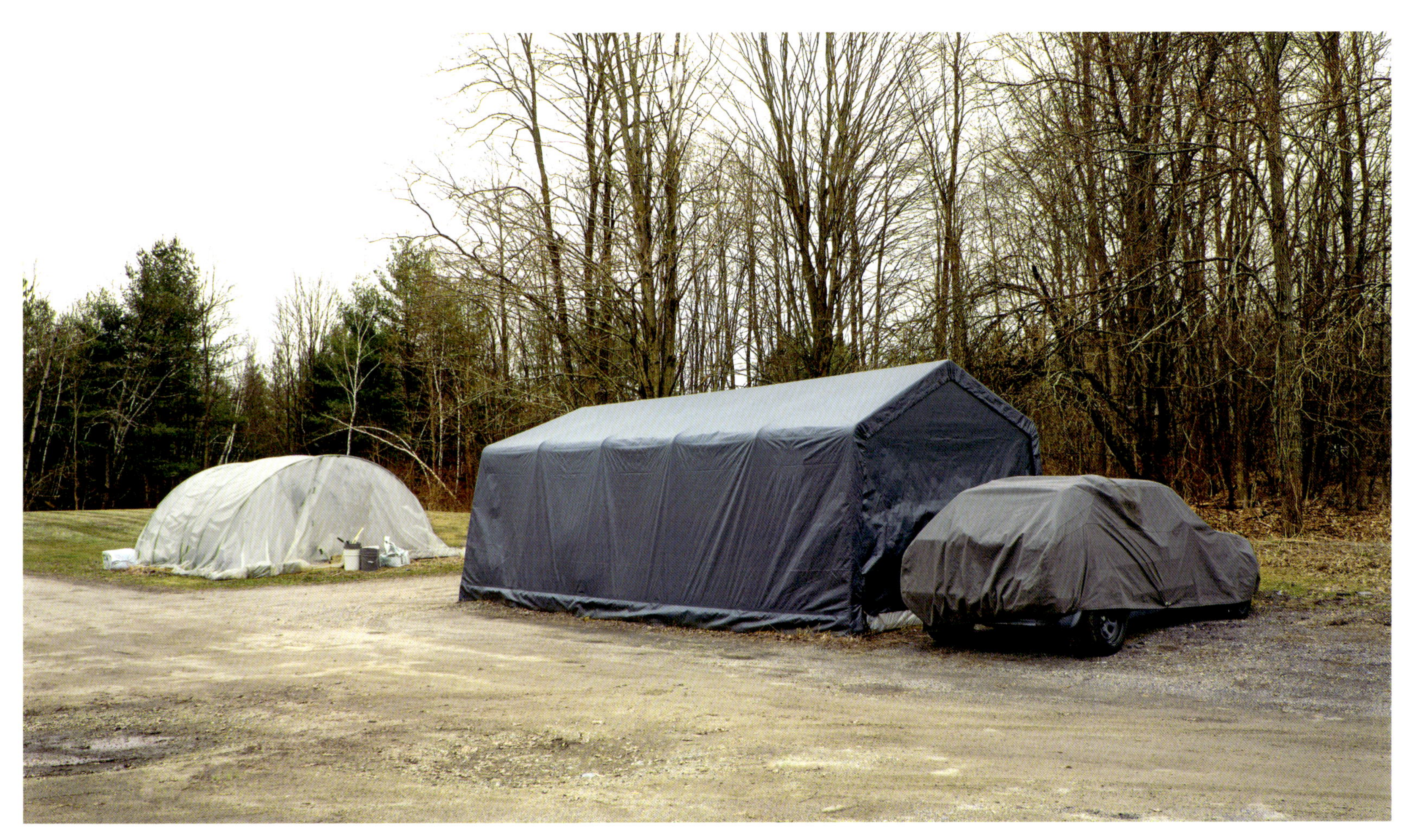

On Sokoki Abenaki homelands. Bernardston, 2018.

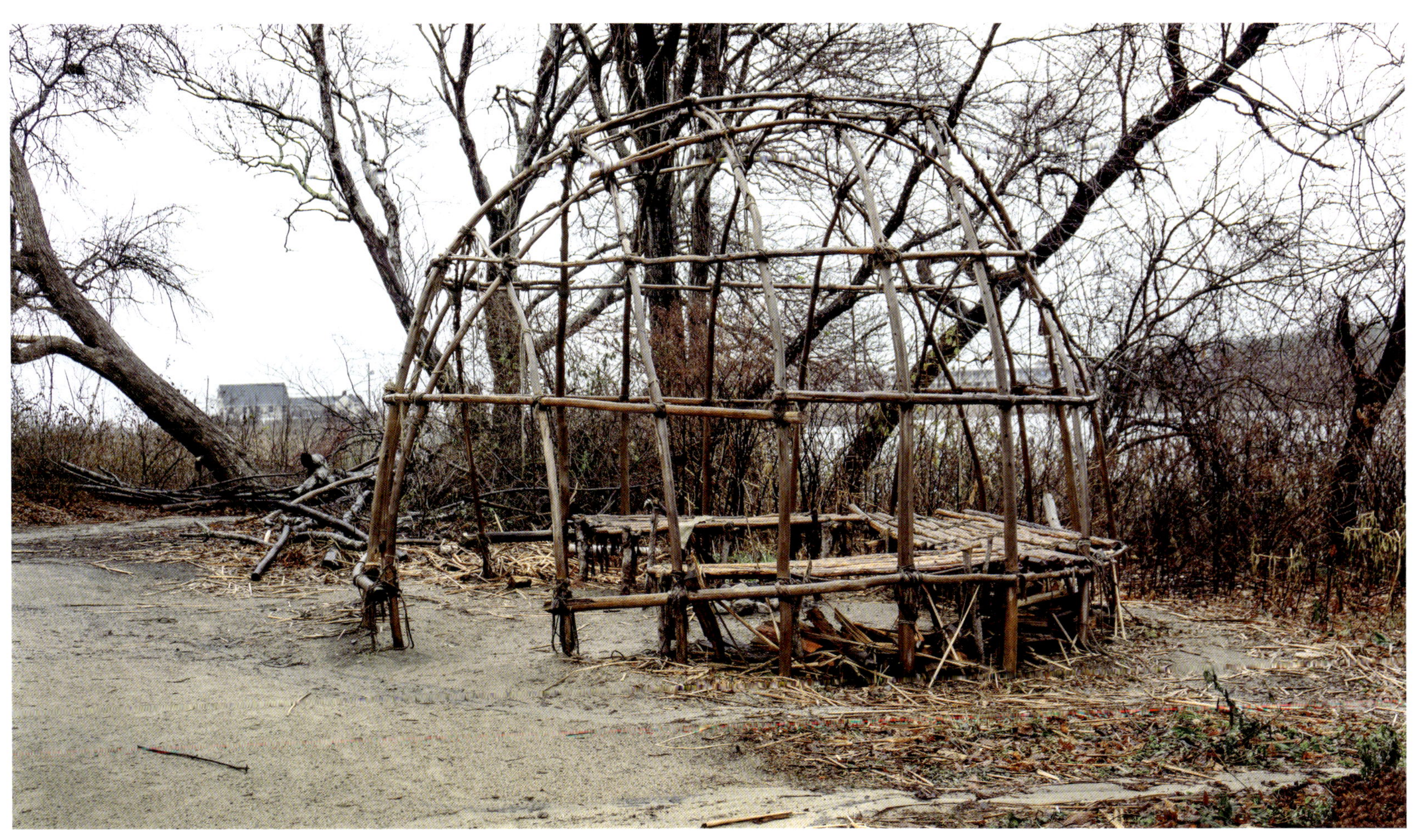

On Wampanoag homelands. A *wetu* frame at Plimoth Patuxet Museums. Plymouth/Patuxet, 2019.

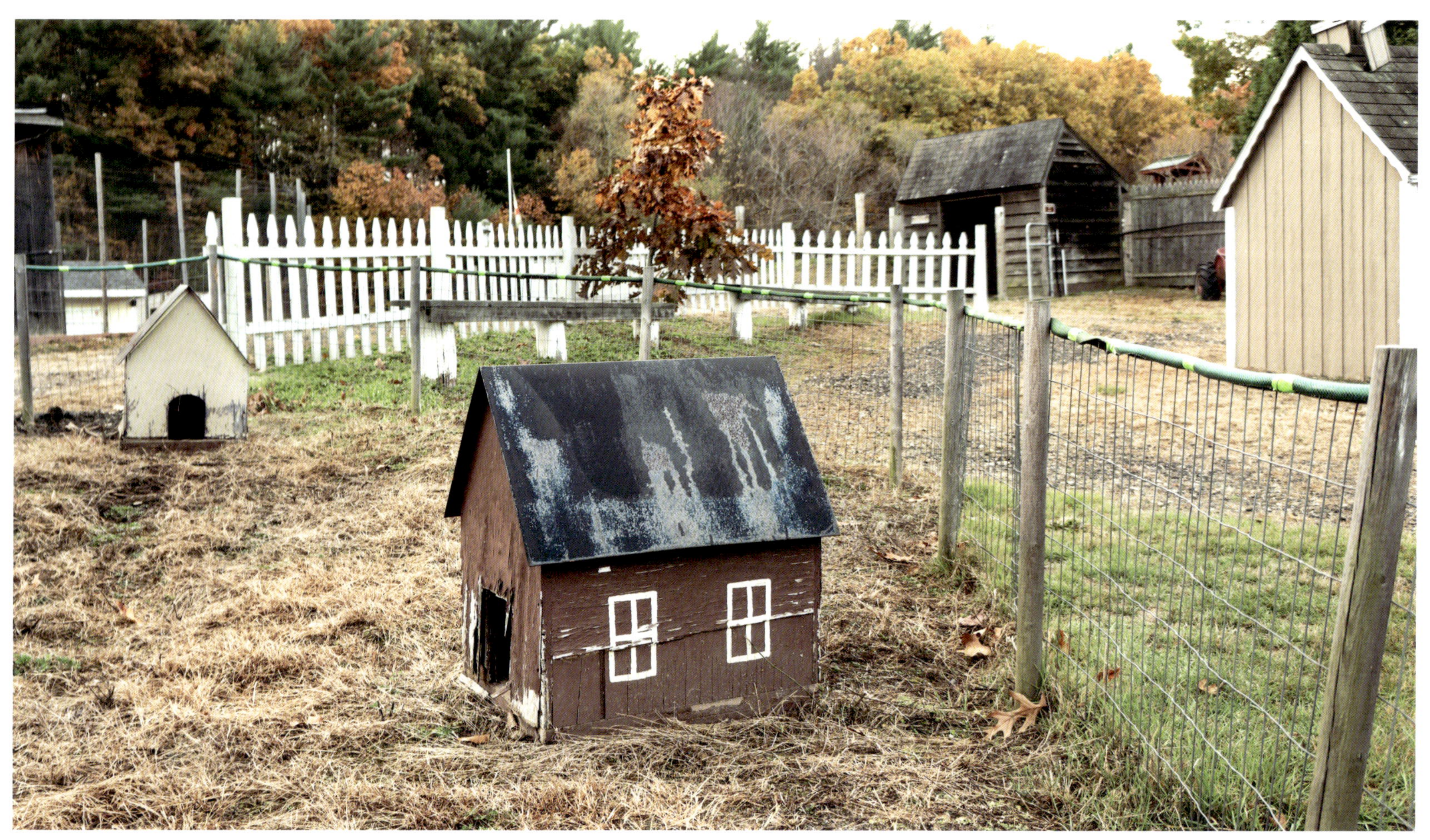

On Nipmuc and Pocumtuck homelands. Rabbit houses. Hadley/Norwottuck, 2019.

Occupying Indigenous Land: Finding a Way Forward

DAVID BRULE

Acknowledging that we occupy land that was taken by force or deception and violence from those who had lived in balance with that land for more than 13,000 years is a first step in trying to heal the injustice.

Yet how do we move forward from such an admission of guilt embodied in a simple acknowledgment of Indigenous land?

The pain is great, the injury has not healed, the multi-generational trauma continues from father and mother, passed on to son and daughter over the ages. Healing is elusive and may well never be complete.

But there are ways that individuals can seek a separate peace, to help a reconciliation process that may well never bring real justice.

Justice and healing will not come through a sweeping proclamation but rather by our individual efforts on a small scale that could build progressively to a new coexistence.

How to create or seize the opportunities knowing that injustices and repression that began more than 400 years ago will never be forgotten, undone, or erased? Indeed, how could Indigenous people ever erase the sight of current devastation the colonizers and colonizing processes are still bringing upon this land?

For Indigenous peoples, the land is alive and populated with an extended kinship among all those inhabiting that land. Native peoples have an intimate relationship with the land, with the stones, mountains, waters, and woodlands, and we are constantly renewing those relationships with the landscape. In Native eyes, these lands should never have been parceled out in allotments of private property. Ever since the forced transfer of the Indigenous landscape during the last 400 years, the relationship has been out of balance and ruled by greed and dominated by the strongest, either individual or corporate. How can there be any reconciliation or healing?

For most of us, all we can do is to start small and continue individually and locally to seek ways to heal.

A case in point: A mixed committee of Tribal and non-Tribal people have been participating in the ongoing study of a particularly brutal massacre of Native elders, women, and children in 1676 during King Philip's War at the site known to Indigenous peoples as Peskeompskut. The site is now named Turners Falls, after the man who led the massacre and who, much like Custer in 1876, paid with his life.

Representatives of five municipalities within whose town boundaries the incidents took place and four Tribes whose ancestors were the victims have been meeting at the same table once a month for six years. These representatives from Montague, Greenfield, Deerfield, Gill, and Northfield and their counterparts from the two Nipmuc/k Nations, the Elnu Abenaki, the Aquinnah Wampanoag, and the Narragansett Indian Tribe have been poring over documents, oral histories, accounts, and archaeologies of the event, doing as best as can be done to find out what really happened. They will then be faced with the challenge of teaching the wider public and finding a way to commemorate the lives that were lost on that fateful day of May 19, 1676.

Beyond exploring the documentation, these individuals are communicating, learning in a subtle, indirect, and implicit way about all those seated around the table and the cultures and histories they embody. Through these Tribal representatives, the Indigenous participants are able to express deeply felt resentments and are hearing their painful memories and generations of trauma being validated by the non-Tribal participants.

At times, some participants in the study who are descendants of the colonial settlers who participated in the atrocity also release and vent their generations-old resentments and prejudices about the Tribal attacks on the fledgling white settlements. Yet through this process of each person being able to tell their side of the story, to share and have that view heard and perhaps validated by the others around the table, and by studying together the different perspectives of the 1676 event, a new implicit understanding is emerging:

> I'd like to think that the memory of this place is being re-examined through this joint town-tribal project for a reason. Working to preserve this site has brought Northeastern tribal descendants and townspeople together again . . . [A]s long as we treat the people

> who perished here with the dignity and respect they didn't receive in life, we will be making some advances towards healing . . .
>
> —Elizabeth James-Perry, Aquinnah Wampanoag historian and member of the Battlefield Advisory Board

To be sure, the occupation of Massachusetts will never end and the wounds of Tribal people are deep and will never be completely healed. Finding a way forward through remembrance, respect, and validation that engenders a new understanding and a new sense of cooperation between Tribal and non-Tribal communities may well be the only way.

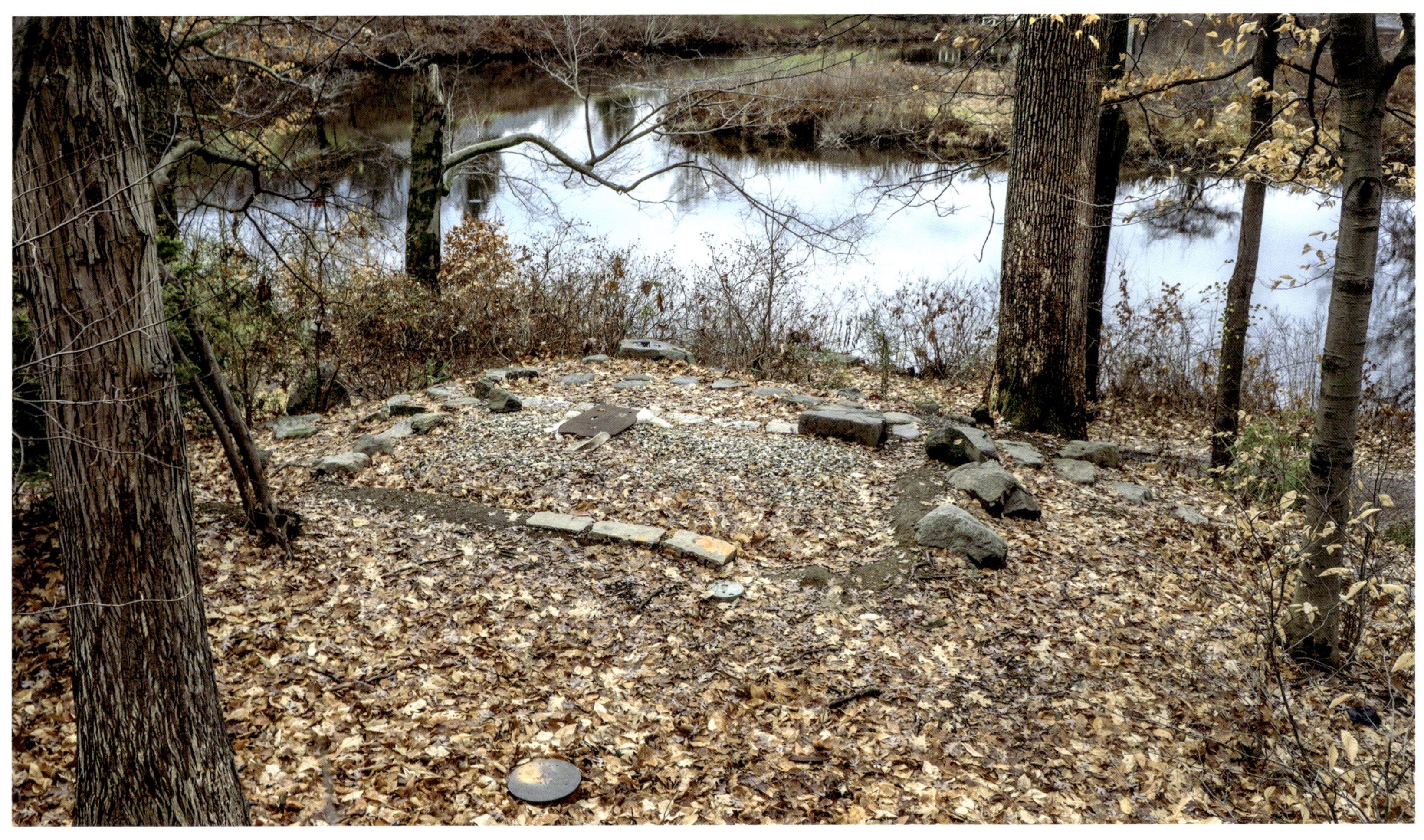

On Nipmuc and Pocumtuck homelands. Remains of a Japanese teahouse overlooking the Mill River, also known as Cappawonganick. Northampton/Nonotuck, 2015.

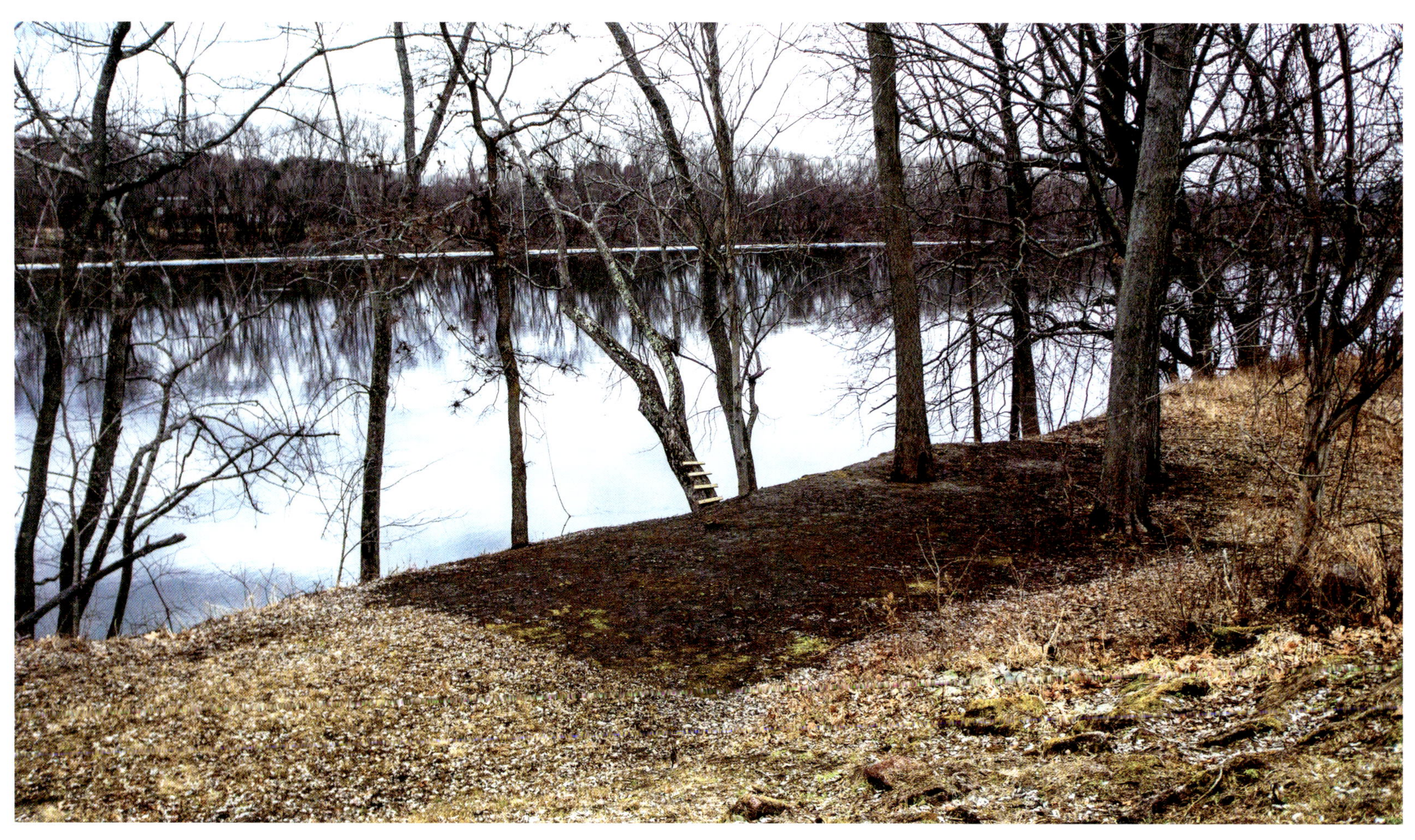

On Nipmuc and Pocumtuck homelands. Connecticut/Kwinitekw River. Hatfield/Capawonk, 2020.

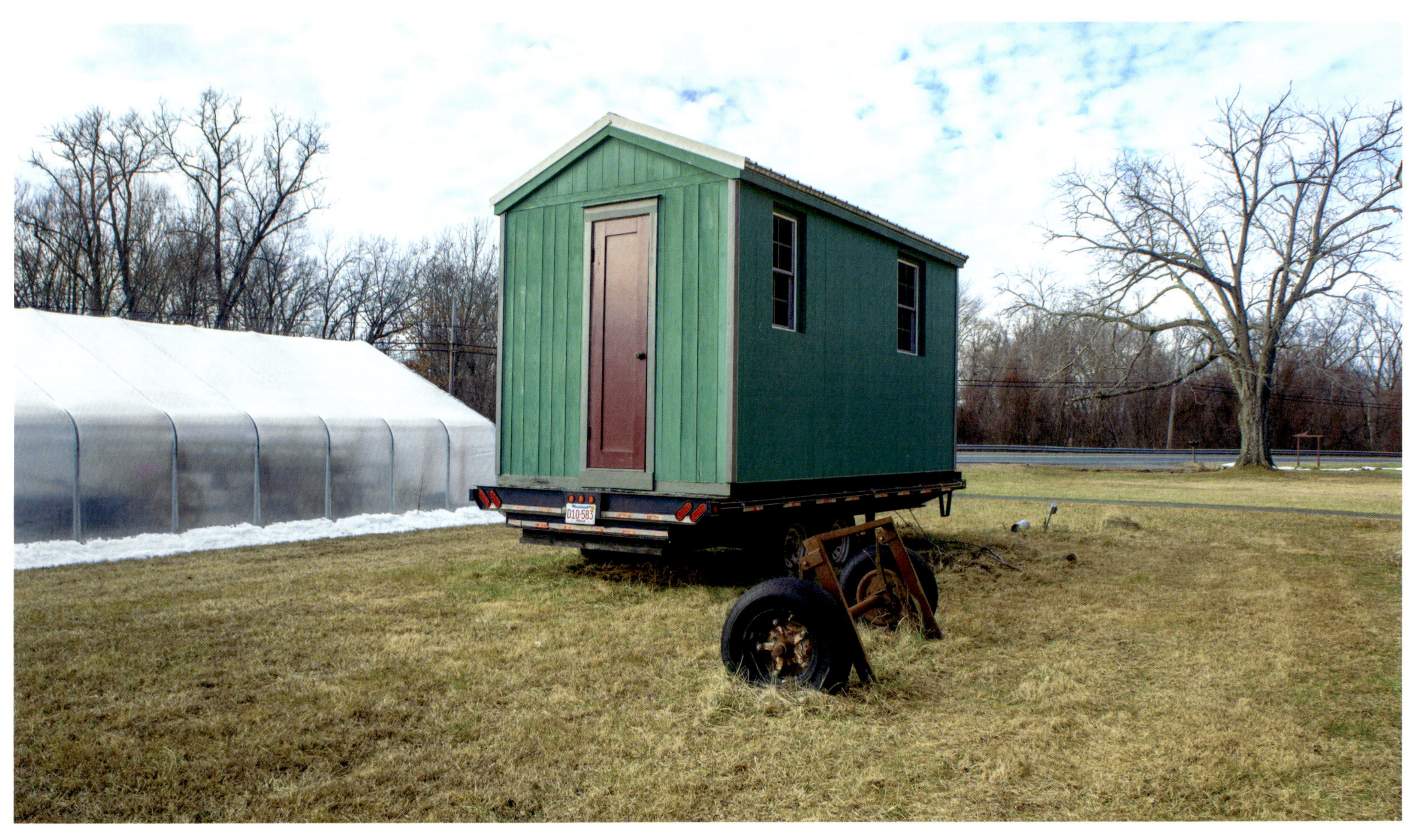

On Nipmuc and Pocumtuck homelands. Hadley/Norwottuck, 2020.

Notes of a Settler Daughter

SUZANNE GARDINIER

1. Bless the Lenape land I'm typing this from. May the repetitions of my ancestors' crimes be interrupted. May we see clearly the paths to interruption of the cycles of repetition and to rebeginning. Bless the imminent post-colonial day.

2. When I look up from typing this, I see a photograph of my grandmother from the back, beside me at one year old, holding something too blurry to see, on a Massachusetts beach called Mattapoisett.

3. Two of the first words I learned to spell: Scituate. Massachusetts. The odd silences I didn't understand, around whose words they were.

4. When I was growing up in Scituate, people sometimes told me I had the map of Ireland all over my face. No one discussed how it happened that the people with the map of Massachusetts all over their faces had "disappeared."

5. Natalie Diaz, from "American Arithmetic" in *Postcolonial Love Poem*: "Native Americans make up less than/1 percent of America./0.8 percent of 100 percent./O, mine efficient country."

6. From Duane Hamilton Hurd in 1884: ". . . human slavery left a larger stain upon the town of Scituate than perhaps upon any other town in this region. Nearly all the families of wealth appear to have owned slaves. At the first these were Indians captured in war, or for some alleged ill conduct reduced to slavery. They captured these human chattels. Later, Africans were introduced, and their freed descendants are numerous in the two towns today. In 1764 there were one hundred and seven African slaves owned in Scituate, and only thirteen Indian slaves."

7. Number of times "slavery in Scituate" was mentioned in my education there: 0. Number of times it's been mentioned in the education of my niece, who lives there and is eleven now: 0. Number of times I heard the word "colonial," with no mention of this aspect of it: past counting.

8. My elementary school was named after a British real-estate speculator, and one year in the annual Thanksgiving pageant celebrating diversity, equity, and inclusion one of my brothers played Squanto, who had one line to say: "Go get fish."

9. In life outside of colonial fantasy, Squanto was Tisquantum, of the Patuxet people, who was kidnapped and sold in Spain by a British captain named Thomas Hunt, who was running his own slave trade. Tisquantum probably spoke both Spanish and English, in addition to his first languages, as he also spent time in London before returning to Massachusetts and finding that white sickness had killed everyone in his village, upon which the *Mayflower* Pilgrim settlers then made their Plantation.

10. "What this town and its surrounding prairie grew from, and what they grew into, is the record of my tribe. If I am native to anything, I am native to this."—Wallace Stegner, *Wolf Willow*, 1962.

11. "It may be that Americans will have to come face to face with the loathsome idea that their invasion of the New World was never a movement of moral courage at all; rather, it was a pseudoreligious and corrupt socioeconomic movement for the possession of resources." —Elizabeth Cook-Lynn, *Why I Can't Read Wallace Stegner and Other Essays*, 1996.

12. How I thought of where I come from—the sun dazzle on the bay, the smell of salt in the rain, the marshes and brooks and inlets, the blaze maples in the fall, and particularly the smell of pine—when I listened to a talk a friend sent a link to: Saidiya Hartman and Fred Moten at Duke in September 2016, talking about "The Black Outdoors." Moten had taught at Duke some years previous and was talking about walking in the woods with his children and how beautiful the land was and is. His little pause before he smiled and said the other part: "I could just always hear somebody running."

13. When I smell pine I still hear somebody running.

14. How the people I was taught to call my people were the people the people were running from.

15. I teach poetry in a prison, around people who are dedicating their lives to finding the paths to life beyond the crimes they've committed, trying to interrupt the cycles of repetition. How many of them are descendants of the people running. How I feel at home there. What "home" means, here in this country.

16. How the Duke discussion series was called "After Property and Possession." How I've spent my life trying to figure out how to get to "after."

17. Just now on Twitter: Laleh Khalili, author of *Time in the Shadows: Confinement in Counterinsurgencies*, commenting on a tweet by Elbridge Colby, whose grandfather ran the CIA's counterinsurgency Phoenix program in Vietnam and who was named after his grandfather's father, who wrote "How To Fight Savage Tribes" for *The American Journal of International Law*, 1927.

17a. First *New York Times* report on what later became known as the My Lai massacre: "GI's, in Pincer Move, Kill 128 in a Daylong Battle" (March 17, 1968).

17b. On the cover of *Life* magazine, four weeks after the massacre: "Vietnam: Burst of Hope" (April 12, 1968).

17c. *Cleveland Plain Dealer* headline (November 20, 1969): "Cameraman Saw GIs Slay 100 Villagers."

17d. *New York Times* (August 25, 1970): "Published reports have described Operation Phoenix as a code name for a secret CIA operation that led to the alleged massacre March 16, 1968. The reports said the CIA had ordered the hamlet wiped out because it was filled with nothing but Vietcong and Communist sympathizers."

17e. Erik Prince on Steve Bannon's radio program, 2016, re Phoenix: "It was a vicious but very effective kill-capture program in Vietnam that destroyed the Viet Cong as a military force. That's what needs to be done to the funders of Islamic terror . . ."

17f. A woman I met at the Shatila refugee camp in Beirut, in the spring of 2002, who'd witnessed the massacre of Palestinian refugees there in 1982: "My son was five years old. I'm sure he remembers. He keeps seeing this, so he remembers. It reminds them of what they saw. How can we forget? Same thing. Same perpetrator. Same method. They are always teaching us to remember. They revise our lesson every day."

17g. A man I met in Gaza at the beginning of 2003, Eyad Sarraj, a psychiatrist who founded the Gaza Community Mental Health Center in 1990: "What is our nightmare? To lose the house. We lost it in 1948. And they keep reminding us. They keep destroying our houses, and they grind salt in our wounds by building their own houses on the ruins of ours." How the Israeli army demolished a hundred and three houses in Gaza that January and killed thirty-seven people.

17h. Eyad Sarraj (1944–2013): "I was born in Be'er Sheva. I still remember the day we had to leave. But I'm ready to give it up for the sake of peace. The children are gods. And no one has the right to kill these gods in the name of God. I want to sacrifice my house in Be'er Sheva. What we need is a world apology and recognition. If we are apologized to, by our honor we have to say yes. But so far we have received bullets and killings and destroying homes instead."

18. In May of 2018 I visited the Massachusetts grave of my ancestor, John Lyman, who in 1676 led the Northampton contingent of the white settlers who raided a camp of sleeping people at dawn, at Peskeompskut or what's now called Turners Falls, and killed the women and children and old people there and threw their bodies in the Connecticut/Kwinitekw River: the My Lai massacre of its day, in the Phoenix program also known as settler colonialism. How every time I hear the words "American values" I think of this.

19. I went with my friend, Arlene Avakian, whom I've known since I was eighteen, who lives in Northampton, on whose mother the whirlwind of genocide descended when she was five years old: "Her father was disappeared, her family sent into exile, the gendarmes took her brother away, and her mother left her and her siblings with relatives to get her son back." —Arlene Avakian and Hourig Attarian, "Imagining our foremothers: Memory and evidence of women victims and survivors of the Armenian genocide: A dialogue," 2015.

20. “Very few of the Indians escaped, and their loss was computed by contemporary writers at three hundred.”—George Madison Bodge, *Soldiers in King Philip’s War*, 1896.

21. How some of the poets in the prison see the rest of their lives as a series of attempts at restitution for what can never be restored.

21a. A friend in New Mexico on my ancestors: “Who’s to say they’re not sorry? Who’s to say they’re not using you to try to make it right?”

22. Nazi-hunter Beate Klarsfeld, in *The Guardian*, 1986: “Because I am a German. Germans have a special responsibility.”

23. Dionne Brand, in *Ossuaries*, 2010: “to undo, to undo and undo and undo this infinitive/ of arrears.”

24. Beate Klarsfeld: “When I learned what happened, I decided that in order not to be ashamed of my people, and to atone for the crimes perpetrated in their name, it was not enough to tell the victims that I merely sympathised.”

25. Adrienne Rich, “From an Old House in America”:

    I try to understand
    he said
    What will you undertake
    she said
    Will you punish me for history
    he said
    What will you undertake
    she said

Note: Sources for the quotes in this essay appear in *Credits* (pages 95–96).

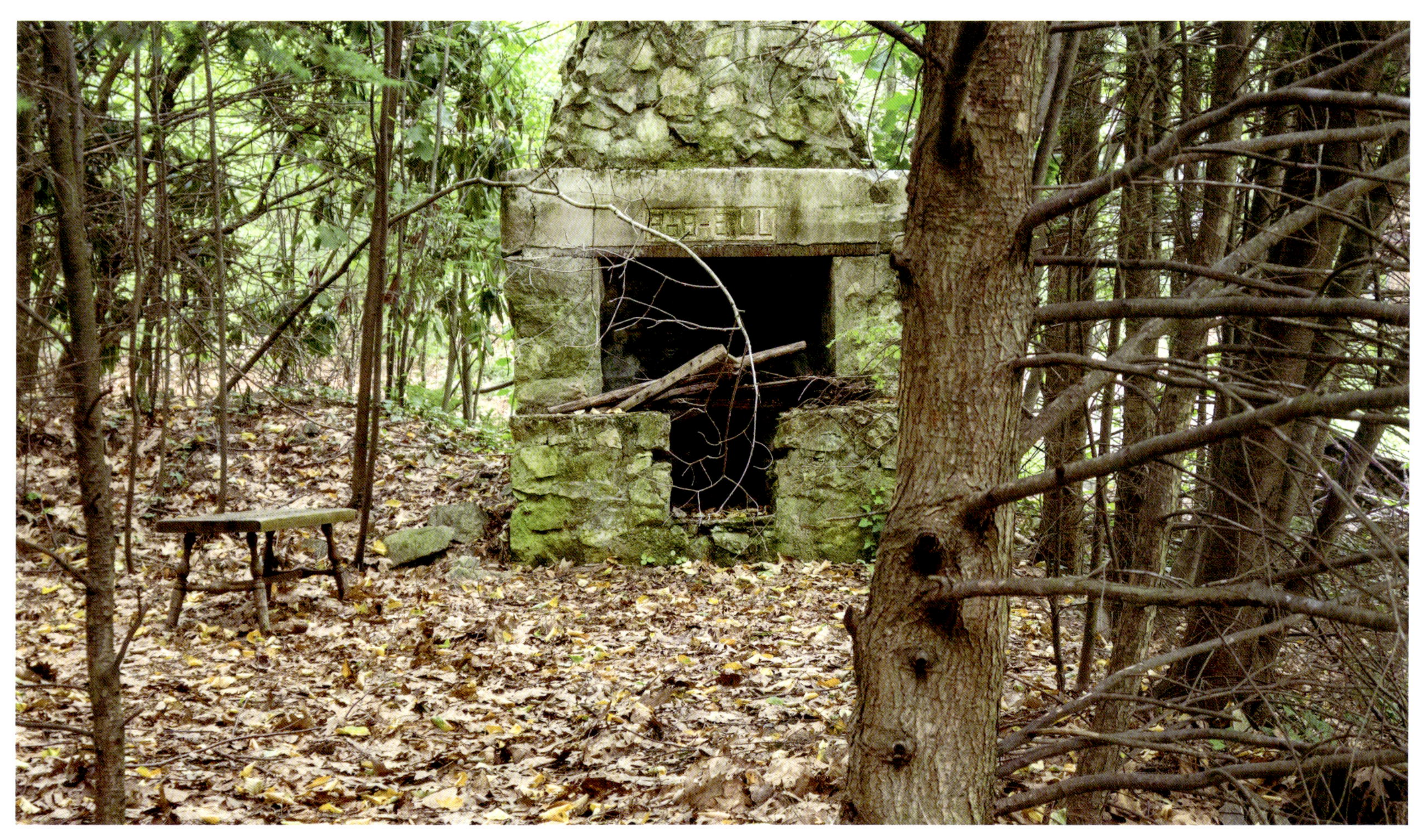

On Nipmuc and Pocumtuck homelands. Northampton/Norwottuck, 2017.

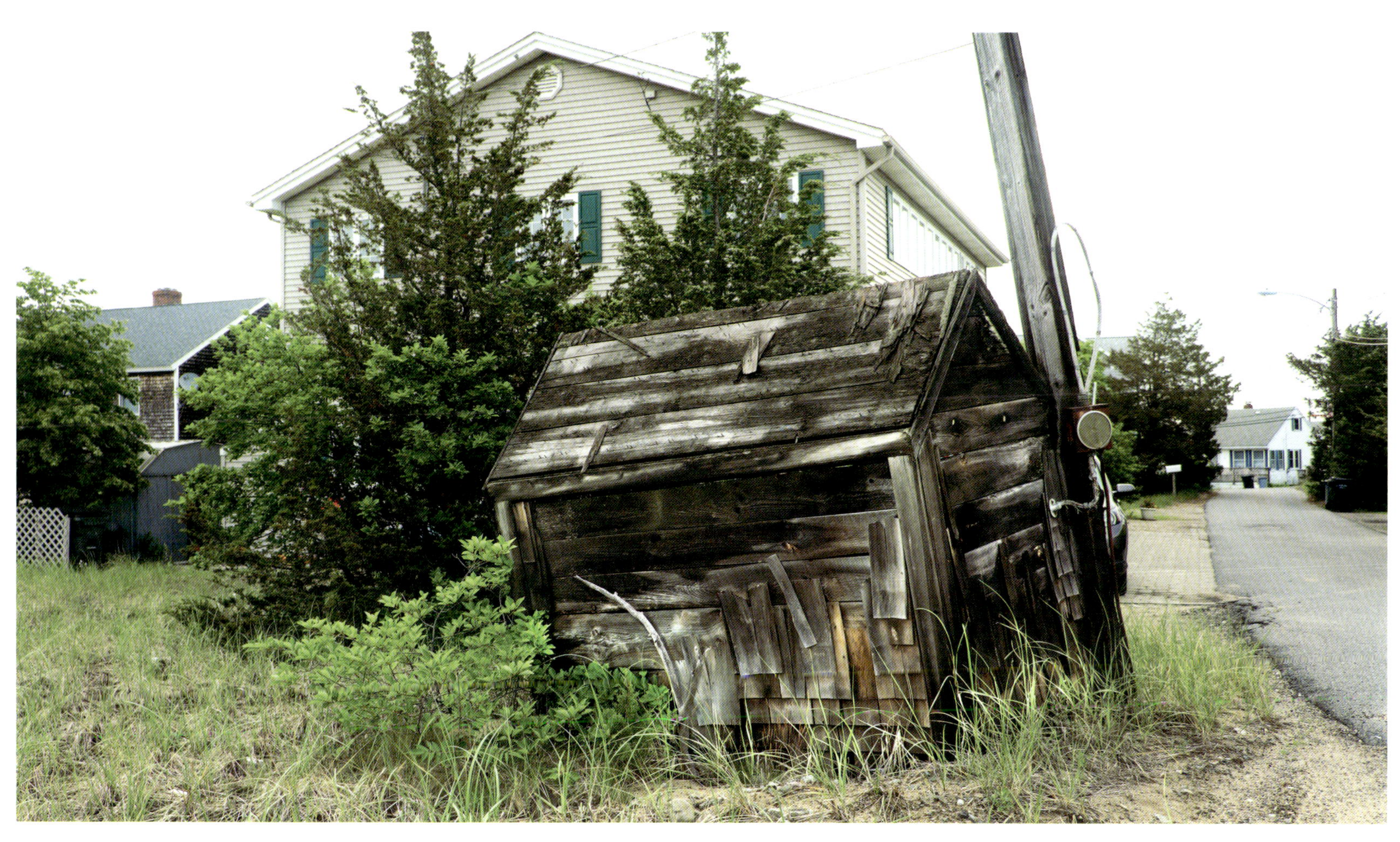

On Pentucket/Pawtucket homelands. Newbury, 2015.

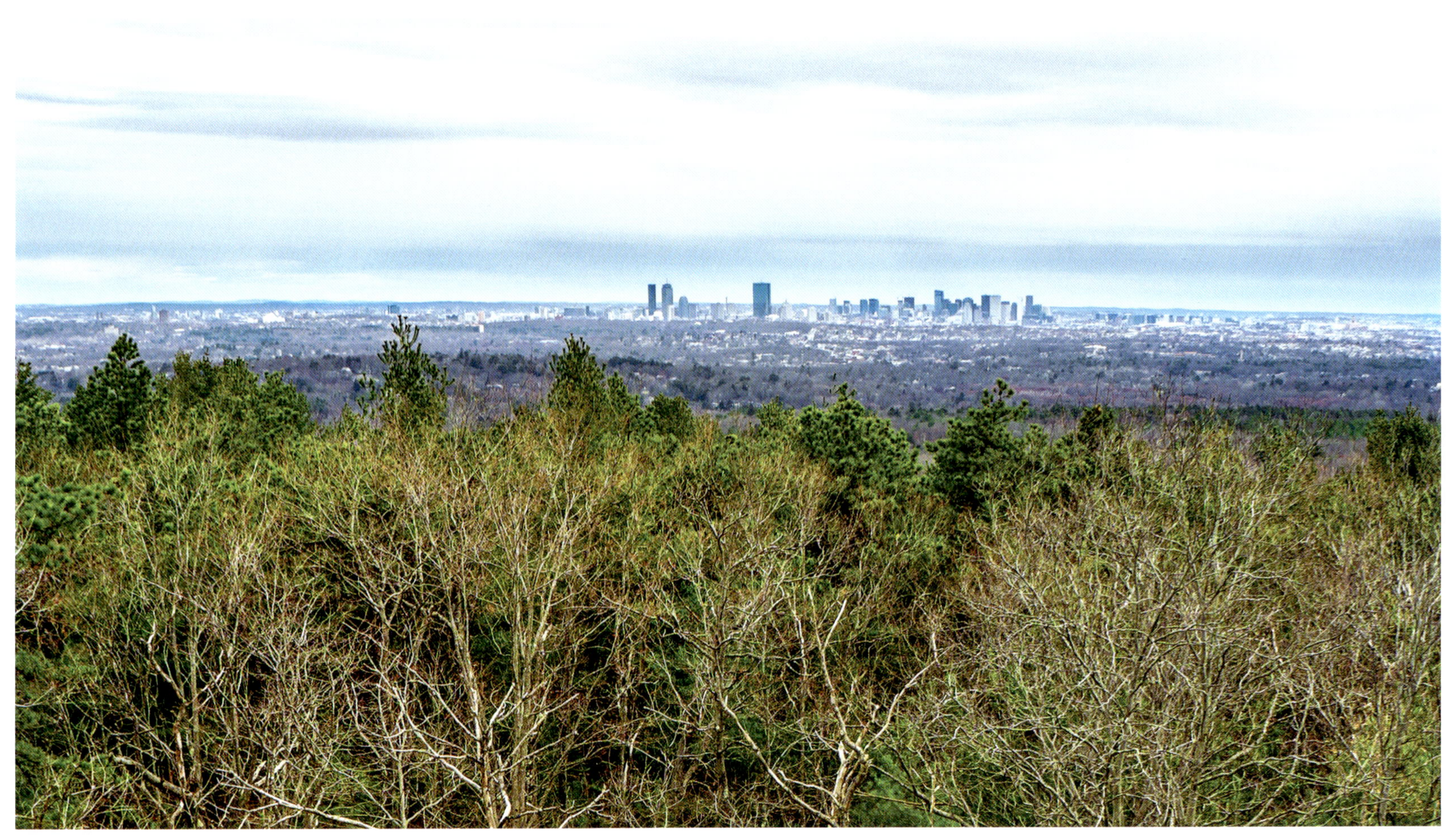

On Massachusett and Wampanoag homelands. View from the Great Blue Hill Observation Tower. Milton, 2021.

MASSACHUSETTS

The name likely derives from either *massa-adchu-es-et* of the Massachusett people or *maswachasut* of the Wampanoag people. Numerous translations exist: "by the blue hill," "at the large hill," "at the little big hill," "at or by the range of hills," "at the large hill place," and "at, near, or about the great hill." Each translation refers to Great Blue Hill (elevation 635 feet/194 meters), the highest point in the Massachusetts Bay region. In 1893, Great Blue Hill became part of Blue Hills Reservation, a 6,165-acre (2,495-hectare) state park some 10 miles (16 kilometers) southwest of downtown Boston.

—Center for the Study of Place (2021)

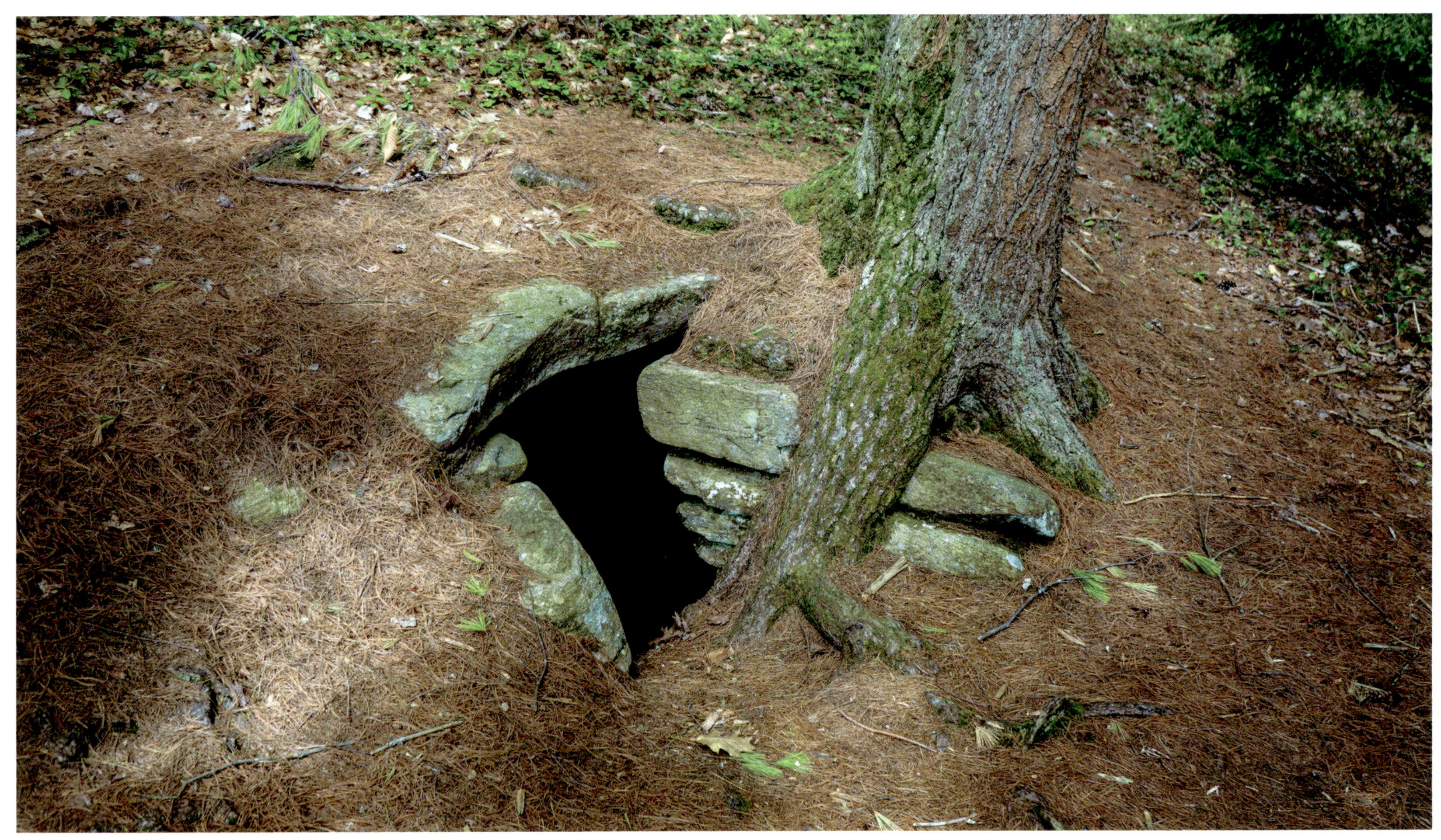

On Nipmuc and Pocumtuck homelands. Entrance to a cylindrical chamber, origin and date unknown. Leverett, 2020.

Notes on Selected Photographs

A note about Indigenous names: Every effort has been made to identify Indigenous homelands and place-names as accurately as possible in all texts, captions, and notes below. Given the complexity of existing information, any errors or omissions are unintended, and corrections and updates are welcome. Indigenous names have been transliterated from spoken languages into the English alphabet in a variety of ways since at least the mid-1600s. The spellings used here and throughout the book have been chosen in consultation with Indigenous sources and are used with acknowledgment that other spellings are also valid.

2/3 The Connecticut/Kwinitekw River, which flows from north to south and bisects Massachusetts, was a major transportation artery for Indigenous groups who have traveled its waters in *mishoonash* (dugout canoes) for centuries. Contemporary Indigenous artist/educators such as Jonathan James Perry (Aquinnah Wampanoag) are reviving the construction, display, and use of *mishoonash.* In 1998, President Bill Clinton designated the Connecticut/Kwinitekw as one of 14 American Heritage Rivers. Mount Sugarloaf/Wequamps, a 210-million-year-old butte-like mountain with two summits (elevation 652–791 feet/199–241 meters), is part of the 533-acre (256-hectare) Mount Sugarloaf Reservation, a state-owned public recreation area. Indigenous stories link its silhouette to the shape and actions of a large beaver.

4 The Pentucket/Pawtucket people were/are part of the larger Pennacook Abenaki group. *Wetuash* is the plural of *wetu* (as mentioned on page 9).

17 This marker and those appearing on pages 21 and 45 are among the nearly 300 cast-iron markers installed throughout the state in 1930 by Massachusetts Bay Colony Tercentenary Commission. The text on the markers was written by Samuel Eliot Morison (1887–1976), a professor of history at Harvard University. The signs all feature a cast and painted image of

the Massachusetts state seal. The seal, adopted first in 1780 and made official in 1885, pictures an anonymous Indigenous man holding a bow in one hand and an arrow—pointed downward to indicate peaceful intent—in the other. Above his head, a disembodied arm wields a broadsword. In 2019/2020, the signs were removed, refurbished, and re-installed by the state, keeping the original texts and design intact, including the seal. In January 2021, after many years of protest, the Massachusetts State Legislature voted to form a special commission to design a new seal, and the measure was signed into law by Republican Governor Charlie Baker.

18 The Parker River, named after Thomas Parker (1595–1677), the Puritan founder of Newbury, is approximately twenty-three miles (thirty-seven kilometers) long and flows through Newbury and adjacent towns into Plum Island Sound and the Atlantic Ocean. In 1942, the Parker River National Wildlife Refuge (4,662 acres/2,287 hectares) was established to provide a safe habitat for migratory birds.

27 The meetinghouse and burial ground were both part of the "Praying Town" of Natick, established in 1651.The land of the "Indian Burial Ground" changed hands several times, and, in 1880, the Bacon Free Library was built on the site. The Natick Historical Society occupies the lower level of the building. There are no marked graves.

30 Maudslay State Park (480 acres/162 hectares) was originally a private country estate encompassing formal gardens, a greenhouse, a working farm, and more than thirty structures to house the family and their staff. Built in 1893 by a wealthy Newburyport family, it was named "Maudsleigh" after the family's ancestral home in England.

31 Goodwin Memorial AME (African Methodist Episcopal) Zion Church was built in 1910, providing a long-term home for an African-American congregation founded in Amherst in 1825.

33 The Agawam people referred to here are connected to the larger Pawtucket group. The Masconomet gravesite is on the grounds of the Sagamore Hill Radio Observatory, a U.S. Air Force facility. Visitors are allowed to enter the grounds, and offerings such as prayer bundles, small sculptures, "dream catchers," and dollar bills can be found at the gravesite.

35 This pathway, adjacent to a Cambodian Buddhist temple, leads to a forest pavilion housing a large statue of a reclining Buddha.

37 Mount Norwottuck (elevation 1,006 feet/337 meters), the highest peak in the traprock/basalt Holyoke Range, appears twice here: at the top of the photograph and again in a painting on the side of a farm building. The mountain was originally named Hilliard Knob but was renamed "Mount Norwottuck" during the mid-nineteenth century by Edward Hitchcock, a professor of geology at Amherst College. Hitchcock was probably unaware that the Algonquian word "norwottuck" translates roughly to "middle of the river." Source: Margaret Bruchac, "Native Presence in Nonotuck and Northampton," in Kerry Buckley, editor, *A Place Called Paradise: Culture and Community in Northampton, Massachusetts, 1654–2004* (Northampton, MA: Historic Northampton, 2004), 18–38.

40 The Hockanum School was built ca. 1853 in what is now called the Hockanum Rural Historic District of Hadley. The building pictured here is adjacent to the school. Mount Holyoke (elevation 935 feet/285 meters) can be seen in the distance. Like Mount Norwottuck on page 37, it is part of the Holyoke Range, which in turn is part of the Metacomet Ridge.

42 The tilting structure is a backyard "sukkah," a temporary ceremonial dwelling built for the Jewish holiday of Sukkot.

53 The Sokoki people were/are part of the larger Abenaki Nation.

57 This commemorative stone has generated protest on several occasions and here shows traces of red spray paint left from an anonymous action in 2011.

60 Ancient ceremonial stone groupings such as the one pictured here can be found in many locations in the Northeast, on both public and private lands. The specific location of this site is deliberately not identified. Efforts to preserve stone groupings often involve collaborations among interested individuals, town governments, and Indigenous organizations. Filmmaker Ted Timreck has made four films—called the "Hidden Landscapes" series—which document research on these ancient stone sites.

61 The spherical chamber, approximately eleven feet (3.4 meters) tall, is reached through a tunnel approximately fourteen feet (4.3 meters) long. Its entrance is thought to be aligned with sunset on the summer solstice.

63 This stone marker and the one on page 71 were installed as a result of an agreement reached in 1998 between the Town of Plymouth and the United American Indians of New England (UAINE). The agreement allows UAINE to conduct a public demonstration/march, without a permit, every Thanksgiving Day from noon to 3:00 p.m. to commemorate the National Day of Mourning.

64 In Shirley, a state-run prison complex was built in 1991 on the grounds of a former Shaker village. The state mandates that the original Shaker buildings be preserved.

65 These tipi-like structures are located outside a business selling Native-made jewelry and other merchandise. Tipis originated among Plains Indians and were not traditionally used by Indigenous people in Massachusetts.

67 This Civil War monument, built on the site of a former colonial fort, links the Civil War with earlier struggles between colonists and Indigenous people. Additional words on the monument expand on this idea: "With pious affection and gratitude, their descendants would hereby associate the sacrifices and sufferings of the fathers of the town in establishing our institutions, with those of their children in defending them."

72 Bernardston was founded by a group of English veterans of the 1676 Battle of Great Falls/Wissatinnewag-Peskeompskut in Gill/Peskeompskut. The land was deeded to them as a reward for having killed more than 300 Native people there, primarily women, children, and elders.

78 The Mill River/Cappawonganick, a tributary to the Connecticut/Kwinitekw River, flows from Goshen to Northampton/Nonotuck. It has changed course several times since the seventeenth century, in response to both natural forces and human interventions.

98 Thomas Cole (1801–1848) made "The Oxbow" a well-known motif in American art in his 1836 oil on canvas painting entitled "View from Mount Holyoke, Northampton, Massachusetts, after a Thunderstorm—The Oxbow."

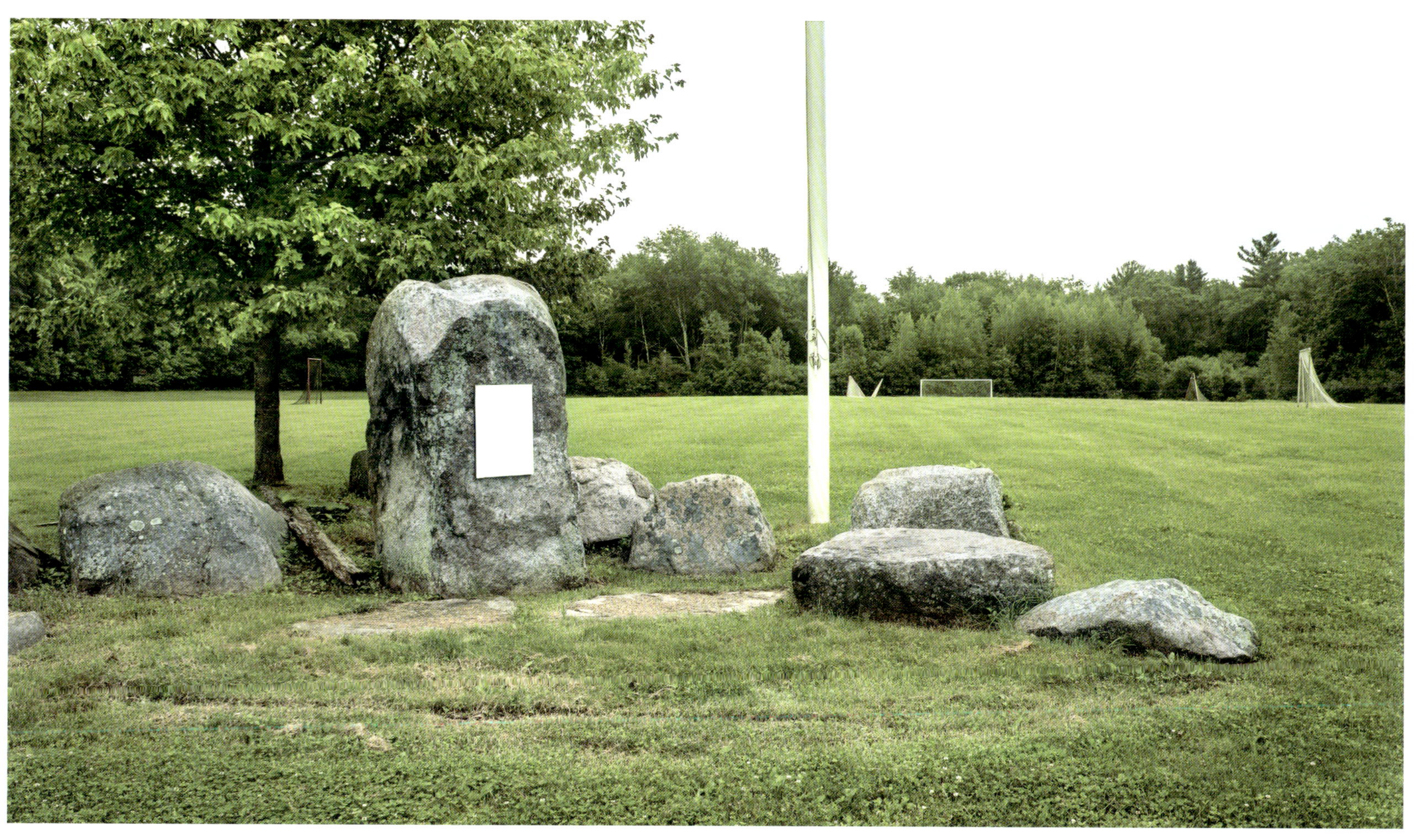

On Agawam/Pentucket/Pawtucket homelands. The text on the marker is concealed under a plastic cover. Hamilton, 2019.

Credits

Text

7 Christine M. DeLucia, *Memory Lands: King Philip's War and the Place of Violence in the Northeast* (New Haven, CT: Yale University Press, 2018), 9.

81 Natalie Diaz, "American Arithmetic," from *Postcolonial Love Poem* (Minneapolis, MN: Graywolf Press, 2020), 17.

Duane Hamilton Hurd, *History of Plymouth County, Massachusetts, with Biographical Sketches of Many of Its Pioneers and Prominent Men* (Philadelphia, PA: J. W. Jewis, 1884), 434.

82 Wallace Stegner, *Wolf Willow: A History, a Story and a Memory of the Last Plains Frontier* (New York, NY: The Viking Press, 1962).

Elizabeth Cook-Lynn, *Why I Can't Read Wallace Stegner and Other Essays: A Tribal Voice* (Madison: University of Wisconsin Press, 1996), 33.

"The Black Outdoors: Fred Moten and Saidiya Hartman in Conversation with J. Kameron Carter and Sarah Jane Cervenak," a public event held on September 23, 2016, at the Franklin Humanities Institute, Duke University, as part of a series entitled "The Black Outdoors: Humanities Futures After Property and Possession." Online at https://www.youtube.com/watch?v=t_tUZ6dybrc.

83 Democracy Now, "The Intercept: Erik Prince Pitched White House Plan for Global Network of Private Spies" (December 6, 2017): https://www.democracynow.org/2017/12/6/headlines/the_intercept_erik_prince_pitched_white_house_plan_for_global_network_of_private_spies.

85 Arlene Avakian, "Imagining our Foremothers: Memory and Evidence of Women Victims and Survivors of the Armenian Genocide," with Hourig Attarian, *European Journal of Women's Studies,* Special Issue on Gendering Genocide, Vol. 22, Issue 4 (May 2015): 476–83; as quoted on 477.

George Madison Bodge, "Soldiers in King Philip's War, being a critical account of that war, with a concise history of the Indian wars of New England from 1620–1677, official lists of the soldiers of Massachusetts colony serving in Philip's War, and sketches of the principal officers, copies of ancient documents and records relating to the war, also lists of the Narragansett grantees of the united colonies, Massachusetts, Plymouth and Connecticut," first issued in the *New England Historical and Genealogical Register,* Volumes 37–45 (1883–1891) and subsequently self-published as a book in Leominster, Massachusetts, in 1896. The quote is from page 246 of that first edition. Slightly updated second and third editions were also self-published by 1906.

Dionne Brand, *Ossuaries* (Toronto, Canada: McClelland and Stewart, 2010), 21.

Beate Klarsfeld, in an article by Polly Toynbee, "Nazi! Nazi!," *The Guardian* (June 16, 1986): 11.

Adrienne Rich, "From an Old House in America," first published in *Amazon Quarterly*, Vol. 2, Issue 3 (March 1974): 38. Used by permission.

Photographs

54/ 73 These photographs of traditional *wetuash* are published with the permission of the Plimoth Patuxet Museums.

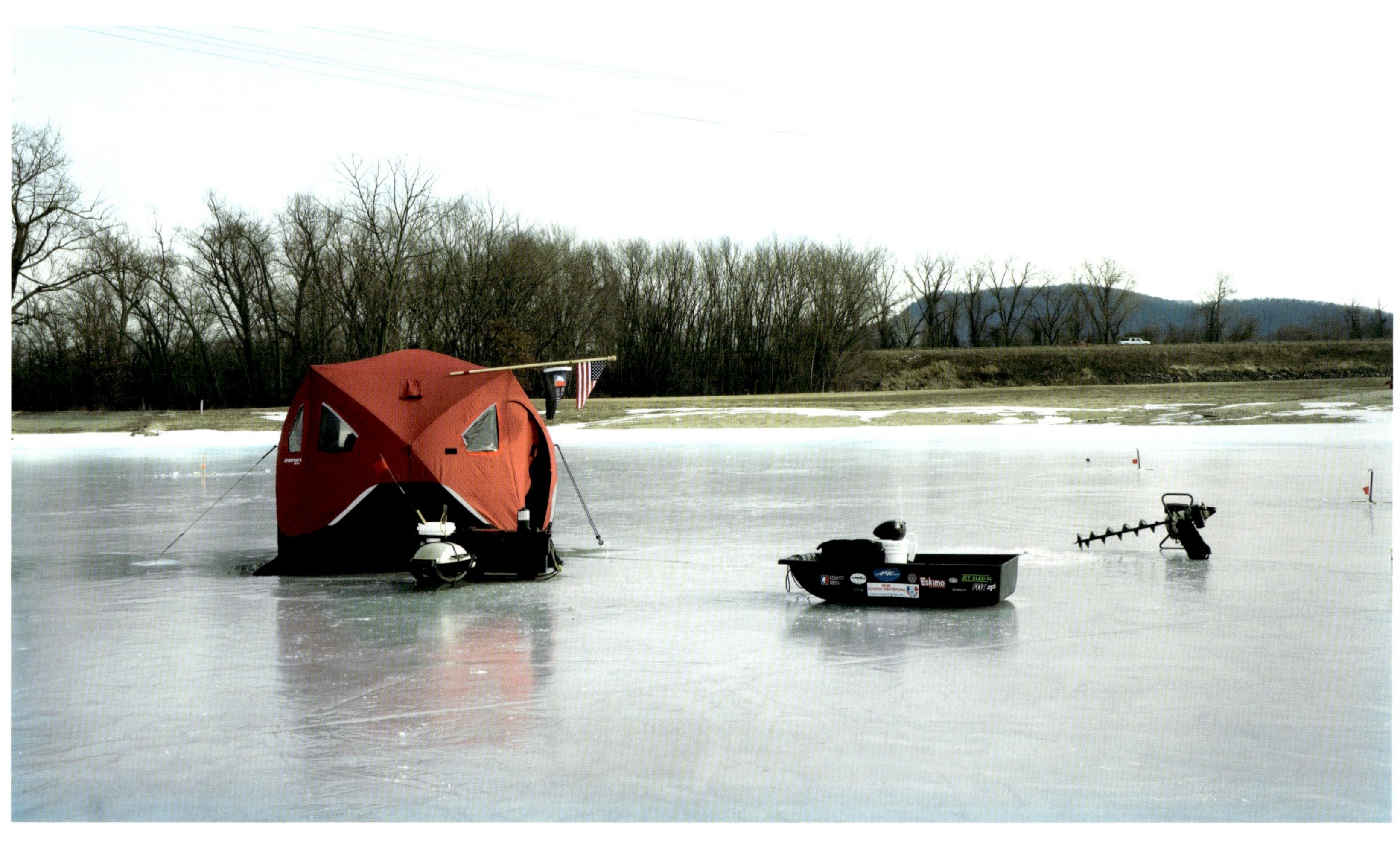

On Nipmuc and Pocumtuck homelands. Mount Holyoke and ice fishing at the Oxbow of the Connecticut/Kwinitekw River. Northhampton/Nonotuck, 2017.

Acknowledgments

The seven-year process of making *Occupying Massachusetts* has profoundly changed how I see my surroundings. Strangely, exploring the complex and painful histories of the state in which I live—as well as the ways in which past events have been suppressed or "spun"—has connected me more deeply to my environment. I can feel the layers of time and the presence of people who lived here centuries ago, and I continue to learn from those who are here today.

In my travels around Massachusetts, many people—friends and strangers—helped me find meaningful locations to photograph. I wish to acknowledge especially the work of Doug Harris—indefatigable champion of ceremonial stone landscapes—and to thank Cathy Taylor, Gary Orlinsky, and Jeri Moran, who guided me to locations I never otherwise would have found.

As the photographs and texts began to come together, I relied repeatedly on the insightful comments of Norbert Goldfield, Matthew Goldfield, Rina Lam Goldfield, Susan Leicher, and Sheila Pinkel, who each looked at multiple versions of the book-in-progress and gave me essential feedback on the project as a whole. Frances Stern, L. Brown Kennedy, and Makeda Best challenged me with key critical perspectives. Rich Holschuh generously guided me with his knowledge of Indigenous cultures and homelands, past and present. Bri Rubero and Stan Sherer expertly worked with me to prepare the images, Eileen Claveloux provided timely technical instruction, and Celeste Jacobs assisted with early design questions. My heartfelt thanks go to these individuals and to many others who lent support, advice, and encouragement along the way.

My work on this book has been buoyed throughout by the vital scholarship of Christine M. DeLucia, Lisa Brooks, Margaret Bruchac, David Treuer, and other researchers who are re-interpreting Indigenous pasts and telling important new stories. Their writings make this a hopeful time for learning about Indigenous histories.

Once *Occupying Massachusetts* was realized in preliminary form, I approached David Brule and Suzanne Gardinier about contributing essays and was enormously thankful when each agreed to write a text. Both contributors are profoundly connected, in different ways, to the massacre of Native people at Great Falls/Wissatinnewag-Peskeompskut on May 19, 1676. Brule grew up near Peskeompskut and led a study group investigating the event, while Gardinier has an ancestor who was one of the perpetrators of the massacre.

Finally, knowing of George F. Thompson's longstanding interest in "American places," I inquired about the possibility of publishing this book with him. I am deeply grateful to George for his help with the sequencing of the photographs and final editorial development of the book; to Mikki Soroczak, for her editorial and research assistance; to Morgan Pfaelzer, for her map of approximate locations of territories used by Indigenous peoples at the time of early European settlement; and to David Skolkin, for bringing *Occupying Massachusetts* so beautifully into existence.

The completion of *Occupying Massachusetts* coincided with the untimely death of Shai Zauderer, my beloved cousin and friend. Shai was an exceedingly generous human, an inspired artist, and a brilliant book designer. This book is dedicated to his memory.

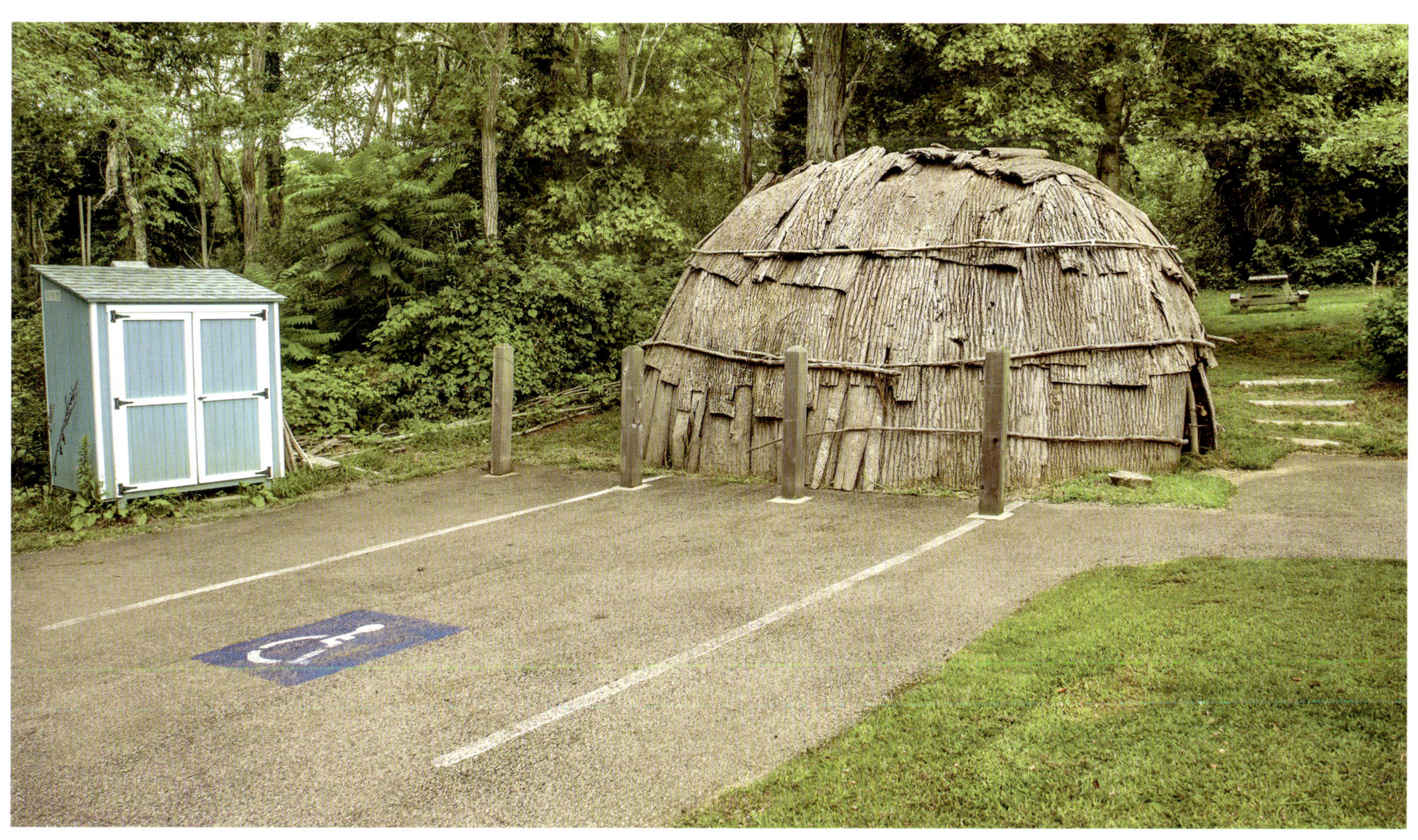

On Wampanoag homelands. A traditional *wetu* on the grounds of the Mashpee Wampanoag Indian Museum. Mashpee, 2019.

About the Essayists

David Brule, who was born and raised in Montague, Massachusetts, is of Nehantic, Narragansett, and Huron/Wendat descent. He is President of the Nolumbeka Project, whose mission is, in part, "to promote a deeper, broader, and more accurate depiction of the history of the Native Americans/American Indians of the Northeast before and during European contact and colonization." The organization works to preserve ancient Indigenous sites in the Connecticut River Valley, offers educational programs, and serves "as a bridge between cultures and between past and future generations." He now lives on Pocumtuck homeland in his great-grandfather's house in Miller's Falls, Massachusetts.

Suzanne Gardinier was born in New Bedford, Massachusetts, grew up in Scituate, Massachusetts, and teaches writing at Sarah Lawrence College. She is the recipient of the Lannan Literary Award for Poetry and the Kenyon Review Award for Excellence in the Essay and the author of twelve books of poetry, fiction, and essays, including *The New World* (University of Pittsburgh Press, 1993), which won the 1992 Associated Writing Program's Award Series in Poetry. Gardinier's work has also appeared in *The Manhattan Review*, *The New Yorker*, *The Paris Review*, and *The Progressive*, among other publications. She currently lives on Lenape homeland in Manhattan.

About the Author

Sandra Matthews was born in New Haven, Connecticut, and resides on Nipmuc and Pocumtuck homelands in Northampton/Nonotuck, Massachusetts. She completed her B.A. in visual and environmental studies at Harvard University and her M.F.A. in photography and film at SUNY Buffalo. From 1982 to 2016, she was a faculty member at Hampshire College. Her previous books are *Present Moments* (self-published, 2020) and *Pregnant Pictures*, co-authored with Laura Wexler (Routledge, 2000). In 2010, she founded the international journal *Trans Asia Photography Review,* which she edited until 2020. Matthews's photographs are in numerous public collections, including the Addison Gallery of American Art, Harvard University Art Museums, Henry Art Gallery, Portland (Oregon) Art Museum, Smith College Museum of Art, Victoria and Albert Museum in London, and Women in Photography International Archive at Yale. Her Website is sandramatthewsprojects.com.

About the Book

Occupying Massachusetts: Layers of History on Indigenous Land was brought to publication in an edition of 850 hardcover copies. The text was set in Century Old Style and Avenir, the paper is Condat Perigord, 170 gsm weight, and the book was professionally printed and bound by Pristone Printing Ltd. in Singapore.

Publisher and Project Director: George F. Thompson

Editorial and Research Assistant: Mikki Soroczak

Manuscript Editor: Purna Makaram

Book Design and Production: David Skolkin

Special Acknowledgments: The publisher extends grateful thanks to John Willis, Bill Press and Elana Auerbach, and Jane and Chops Wong, for their generous support of this book.

Published in 2022. First hardcover edition.
Printed in Singapore on acid-free paper.

George F. Thompson Publishing, L.L.C.
217 Oak Ridge Circle
Staunton, VA 24401–3511, U.S.A.

www.gftbooks.com

30 29 28 27 26 25 24 23 22   1 2 3 4 5

The Library of Congress Preassigned Control Number is 2021947745.

ISBN: 978–1–938086–89–2

Front endpaper image: "Connecticut River Oxbow." Data sets: SIO, NOAA, U.S. Navy, NGA, GEBCO, Image Landsat/Copernicus, Image U.S. Geological Survey. October 4, 2018. 42° 24′ 36.92″ N, 72° 32′ 04.84″W, eye altitude 13.48 miles. http://www.earth.google.com (December 8, 2021).

Back endpaper image: "Newburyport area." Data sets: SIO, NOAA, U.S. Navy, NGA, GEBCO, October 10, 2020. 42° 50′ 13.84″ N, 70° 51′ 11.63″ W, eye altitude 39,494 feet. http://www.earth.google.com (December 6, 2021).

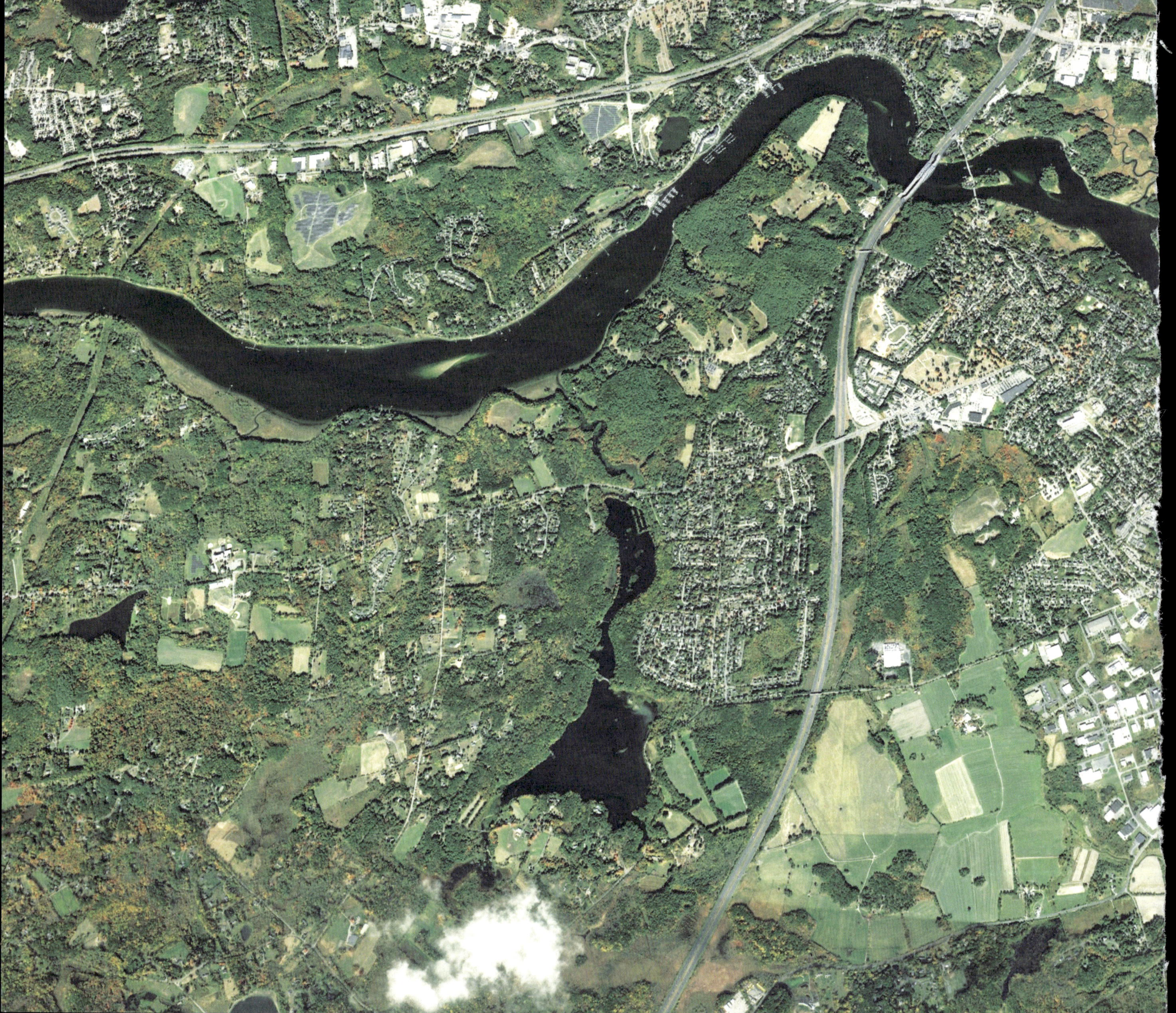